Pontius Pilate and His Gospel of Jesus

A Tale of the Christ

By Michael E. Morgan

Copyright (c)2008 by Michael E. Morgan

All rights reserved, including the right to reproduce this work in any form whatsoever, without permission in writing from the author, except for brief passages in connection with a review.

For information write to:
Crazyfox Publications, LLC
P.O. Box 13
Bronxville, NY 10708-9998
Or call: {914) 274 - 8352

If you are unable to order this book from your Local bookseller, or Amazon.com, you may order directly from the publisher.
Quantity discounts for organizations are available.

ISBN 09662397 - 0 - 9 (paper)
10 9 8 7 6 5 4 3 2 1

Printed on acid free paper in Canada

Crazyfox Publications, LLC

Crazyfox Publications, LLC formed in New York State in 2006 to facilitate the spreading of spiritual truths and wisdom in books for all of the people in the world at a time when little of what would be called wisdom still exists. The world has grown harsh, crass and bent on materialistic pursuits. With saber rattling and actual military conflicts raging, the instability of financial and political systems threatens life as we know it. There is little for anyone to count on in the way of real support and the all but forgotten sense of the real meaning of life as well as the heart felt values that were once held in high esteem.

Crazyfox Publications LLC is 'crazy like a fox' seeking after the lost and buried treasures that still exist in the world and serves to refresh the public mind of what is worth seeking after, the true adventures of the exaltation of the spirit through that which is written down in books which may offer hope for a better life here on Earth.

About the Author

Michael Morgan has been a successful electronics engineer in the television broadcasting industry for more than forty years merging a unique combination of artistic talent with his technical knowledge. At the age of twenty eight he had a profound spiritual experience which changed his life. He read many books on spirituality and philosophy, and spent fifteen years engaged with Reichian bio-energetic therapy. Then another twenty years in the practice of Yoga and tutored by a Taoist Master. During that time, he also studied with secret brotherhoods in both America and Peru which continued to enhance his meditative spiritual skills.

In 1985 he had a near death experience which precipitated a strong psychic connection with spirit and learned to draw upon those paranormal resources and shared the knowledge and wisdom he received with the world. Later, he was invited to Japan where he spent three years lecturing and giving seminars on a range of spiritual subjects and led several large groups on tours to Egypt and Greece introducing them to the ancient cultures of the Egyptian and Greek mystical traditions.

In 1987 Morgan wrote his first book, The Emerald Covenant, published by Hampton Rhodes detailing his journeys and adventures to these mystical places. For years after, he continued his writing and went on to publish several short stories through the Ford Group with Dutton under the heading of Hot Chocolate for the Mystical Soul series.

Through his spiritual guide, Morgan continues to learn new spiritual skills in which, he continues to write stories which define his own brand of spiritual adventure and passion such as his latest work, Pontius Pilate and His Gospel of Jesus, A Tale of the Christ.

Morgan founded Crazyfox Publications, LLC, in 2006, an On Demand Publishing organization working through Ingram's outsourcing firm Lightning Source, Inc., to facilitate the continued dissemination of his stories and ongoing adventures. Michael Morgan presently lives in New York working as an engineer and continues to write books about personal transformation, and chronicles in this process, his own development, knowledge and experiences.

Preface

The truth is there were really two churches in the early Christian movement. The original church founded in 31 AD by the Disciples of Christ in Jerusalem and the other church founded in Asia by Paul and in Rome by Simon Magus, the false prophet to the gentiles in 67 AD. In Acts, Luke warns about the church in Rome and makes several ominous references to this church rising almost simultaneously with the little church in Jerusalem.

The Roman Church looked to expand its influence and increase its power base with other pagan religions in Europe and Asia. Whereas not much survived from the original Jerusalem church's writings regarding what really happened after the end of Jesus' ministry. After Paul's death, the surviving Roman Church led by Simon Magus made sure the story was told a certain way which made Jesus a deity, emphasized his death, and integrated many pagan rituals into its doctrine which had nothing to do with the original Christian movement.

In the fourth century AD the Roman Church led an ecumenical purging of all of the gospels. Before the ecumenical purging there were many stories, gospels if you will, about those who had an experience of the Christ. The Roman Church needed the gospels to agree in content and follow its agenda. They needed a deity in Jesus to challenge the deities of the pagans in other lands if they were to secure converts and their wealth. Therefore, out of all that were discarded as heretical, they chose the four that we know, Matthew, Mark, Luke, and John, which were then modified until essentially concordant.

Of primary importance is what the Christ taught about life and how to live it. It was not about death. The author believes that Jesus was the symbol of resurrection; an awakening from the death of unconscious life to a new conscious and deliberate life of love, compassion and understanding, which embraces a life beyond this illusory world. Perhaps it was not so important that he was not born of an immaculate birth, or that he did not die on the cross. It does not lessen the importance of the prophet and his message. He demonstrated God's will on the earth and a new way to live. Equally important, He showed us how to address God directly without the need for intercessors.

The Greek Orthodox Church always believed He was a prophet, not a deity. It was more important that he be born a man that God saw fit to be Christ. He was a great prophet and had the power for a short time to prove, through the miracles he performed, the reality of God's power on earth. God brought him on the earth to teach us a new way of morality, goodness, and greater self-responsibility.

One other significant aspect in this version is Jesus' loss of God's Witness, or the Christ Consciousness. Why would God take that away in Jesus' hour of need and then allow him to experience all of that torture? Jesus did not only come here to teach us the truth, but through his life experience he demonstrated a way for us to return to God's grace. In the fall from grace it is our righteous indignation and rejection of God's way that puts us into the darkness and ejects us from the metaphorical 'garden' from the beginning. It is fitting that we have to work our way back through our suffering without the benefit of God's witness to help us. That said, we would regain our love and respect for God and abide by his will not because we fear him, but because we want to.

The author believes Jesus' path of suffering is our path of suffering. In some sense, he ultimately died for our sins; not to eliminate them, but to show us the need for humility and remorse. Jesus declares that it is God's will to be done, not our will to be done. As the prodigal son learns from wasting his father's inheritance, he realizes he is better off returning as a servant of his father rather than starve in the wilderness as a lost son. In addition, it is important to note that the father in that allegory rejoices for his son's choice to return home. Also note, the father's acceptance indicates an assurance of a return to grace.

Also interesting to note is the depiction of the original apostles' loving relationship with Jesus and with each other according to the Roman church. In Pilate's version, you see their relationship not so loving, often argumentative, hostile, and even self-serving. Perhaps this is more honest from a human perspective and perhaps easier to accept. It indicates how difficult it was for them to accept change and begin a new way of life while giving up their former lives and families to take on a dangerous and important mission.

Each one of us has our own perspective of life here on the earth. When we die, we leave an impression of our feelings and thoughts behind stored within a living substance called the Akasha. The Akasha is part of the energy that surrounds and binds all life together called the Life Force. Western spiritual traditions do not know or teach this idea but it is common knowledge in Eastern spiritual traditions.

For more than twenty years, I have been under the tutelage of an ascended master called Yokar. He is my personal spiritual guide and inner teacher.

Over the years, he taught me many spiritual skills and widened my understanding of life and the universe. One of those skills is the ability to read the Akashic records, which allowed me to develop this story.

Pontius Pilate's perspective reflects history from a point of view that does not have an agenda. We can then embrace what Pilate experienced as a practical and less exaggerated version of the story. This version also reveals conversations beyond the assertions by the Roman Church.

We need to ask what were the real underlying reasons behind Pilate's reticence to convict the Nazarene. Learn first hand from the one who was actually there.

It makes sense that Pontius Pilate met several times with the one called Jesus of Nazareth, The Christ. Even if those meetings may have only had the purpose of determining the rightfulness of his conviction, what kind of discussions might they have had to make Pilate question the whole idea of his conviction and crucifixion?

The point of this book is to show how a practical man, a soldier of Rome, was changed by the revelations of one of the greatest men the world has ever seen, a renegade rabbi and prophet, a true visionary who came to show us a new way. The importance of what this man taught may not have survived the ravages of time, or the agendas of greedy and powerful men. Perhaps the truth emerges in its own way, ultimately because like life, it is tenacious, and by divine will, finds its way into the hearts of men and women even though it might appear as just another story.

Michael E. Morgan

Content

Prologue			13
Chapter	1	Governor Pilate	16
Chapter	2	Revolt in the Streets	30
Chapter	3	The Nazarene Returns	41
Chapter	4	The Blind and the Dead	50
Chapter	5	Caiaphas and the Counsel	60
Chapter	6	John Baptizes Jesus	65
Chapter	7	Saul's Gambit	76
Chapter	8	Paul and the disciples	81
Chapter	9	Jeshua Weds Mary	90
Chapter	10	Jeshua's Temptation	95
Chapter	11	First Meeting	105
Chapter	12	Peter Verses Mary	117
Chapter	13	Further Dialogues	125
Chapter	14	In Herod's Court	134
Chapter	15	The Warning	139
Chapter	16	The Last Stand	151
Chapter	17	Judas' Betrayal	161
Chapter	18	The Trial	174
Chapter	19	Pilate's Gambit	186
Chapter	20	In View of Golgotha	199
Chapter	21	Mary's Vision	208
Chapter	22	Paul's Challenge	221
Chapter	23	Peter's Second Betrayal	227
Chapter	24	Caligula's Justice	237
Epilogue			242

Prologue

It is always dry in Judea, parching the throat and searing the nostrils at every waking moment. It is maddening really. Perhaps this suggests a reason for the relentless unrest that permeates this country. It prompted my immediate request of the palace servants to supply me with freshly poured wine whenever needed.

Herod's servants are pleasant to look at. Their beauty and fragrance are often reminiscent of Roman women. Sometimes they distract my concentration. Depending on his mood, Herod will often surround himself with delicate and succulent females. Then he secretly allows his eyes to wander and want.

As the procurator of Judea, they also cater to me. In addition, as the Governor of Judea, I keep the peace, but I long for more. The thought of Herod's throne is seductive and delights my senses. Since my arrival, the king's agitation over my presence seems obvious. Our mutual lust for greater power enhances our potential to compete. Our friendship is complicated and builds upon his desire to keep peace with Rome and a closer watchful eye on a new threat,

Rome's new governor of Judea. His paranoia and fear of the loss of his throne goes with him to his bed every night.

When I first learned of my new assignment from Tiberius, my friends in Rome could not decide whether to congratulate or console me. My closest advocate, Sejanus, seemed all but enthusiastic about my prospects. Many tribunes know that governing Judea is unwieldy and the worst of all charges. My predecessor, Valerius Gratus, would attest to the challenge, and he lasted only a short time.

This leaves me to wonder. Was this assignment a punishment for some indiscretion on my part, or an opportunity to rise to greater importance on my return to Rome? If it were to be the first choice, then a man fit of mind would consider rejecting Tiberius' proposal and flee quickly to Capri. However, being mentally fit I find rejecting the emperor's request not to be an option. Such sympathies are not common for the emperor Tiberius. He would certainly make the legacy of my career shorter than expected.

I did not come this far by the favor of the Gods, but I shall not deny the Gods their place in all manner of things, nor will they find me arrogant to exclude them. It is my firm belief that I am at this station mostly through my cleverness and keen sense of the body politic. So instead, I choose to believe the emperor's choice is for loftier purposes.

The zealots, prophets, and messiahs are at every corner. Their many voices lift up through the constant howl of the wind blown streets and sand filled air. Their cries are for deliverance from those of us who look down upon them with a certain measure of superiority. The governor is Rome and with that, I am not welcome here. However, I am well accustomed to the chill of an enemy's flank, so as I lift up my cup I drink to all the misfits. I say to myself that this station suits me just fine. It actually makes my job easier. I can dispense with all of the pleasantries of municipal gallantry. I will ensure they feel the power of this Roman's blade and all will know it.

Perhaps Gratus was too weak to keep order here. Make no mistake Judea, I will be the first that will wield power and strength over you without mercy, limiting your freedom, while I declare the uselessness of such hopes of inflamed injustices. The swords of my well-trained garrison will be tempered and seasoned with the blood of your seditionists.

Governor Pilate

Two manservants appeared at the entrance to Pontius Pilate's quarters. They approached quietly so as not to disturb him, but Pilate's keen sense of hearing made their footsteps heard well before they ascended the winding staircase. He faced them and demanded, "Yes, what is it?"

The servants recoiled. "We beg pardon of you, great one. King Herod requests your presence at the celebration."

"Does he now? We do not want to disappoint the Great Herod. I graciously accept his offer. Go quickly, lest you upset your master by delaying too much. Tell him we shall be along shortly."

They stretched their arms and hands to offer him their respect. "As you wish, great one."

Pilate paused to consider what he was going to do. He looked at his wardrobe and chose the tunic with the white breastplate. The descent down the stone staircase gave Pilate time to reconsider his conceit. He entered one of the four arched passageways that led to the Great Hall, and music and cheers filled the air. The noise assaulted the calm he had achieved in the quiet of his quarters.

The hall sat almost central to the palace. Before him was a series of white marble ring steps, giving him the sense he was entering a great stone bowl. Veiled nude dancers leaped before him. They swayed to the music in and out of the center arena.

Steps ended at the cream-colored marble floor that stretched to the other side and gave the impression of great opulence. Another set of ring steps ascended to where King Herod sprawled across his settee, wrapped in gold and purple silk lined robes of linen. Next to him sat his brother's former wife, Herodias, now his wife. She stared at Herod with a beguiling smile to hide her intolerance for his many female admirers. Courtesans, friends, heads of state, and perhaps some enemies, reclined about the circle between lavish platters of food and wine.

Thick pillars circumscribed the space and exotic incense scented the air. Pilate swooned from the pleasure of his senses. Herod's laughter rose above the roar of the crowd and captivated Pilate's attention long enough to see the king motion him to sit nearby. Pilate navigated his way carefully through the gyrating women to seek a place to sit.

To the left of Herod lay a pile of partially rolled carpets. As Pilate began to sit, Herod frowned at Gaius Aurelius, the older praetorian from Syria. Gaius jumped at the king's silent command to exchange his settee for the carpets. Herod encouraged Pilate to accept the gift of the luxurious settee. Pilate nodded and smiled. Gaius returned his nod sheepishly, not expecting Pilate's display of humility.

Herod smiled broadly. He gestured and spoke while chewing on a leg of lamb he held in his hand. "Please, my dear friend, relax. You look tired and weary. Allow my hospitality to loosen your spirit." He beckoned to his servants. "Give the Procurator a cup filled with my best wine and have him drink his fill. Tonight he shall know the bounty of Herod's court."

Pilate nodded to the king. He looked at Herodias and wondered if under her robes she held a treacherous dagger. Their relationship was not born of love, but lust and political gain.

Night wore on into the early hours and the music becalmed and the dancing subsided. Many fell asleep from too much drink, and remnants of their supper stained the clothing of those they intertwined with. The nose quickly forgot the fragrance of incense and beheld the sour smell of undigested food.

Pilate settled into numb sobriety. He did not take to excess, stemming from his training as a soldier in which he learned to get along without many of the luxuries of Rome while on long campaigns against the people of Gaul. The severity strengthened his resolve to win many of the battles he commanded for the honor of Rome.

Herodias felt the king's desire for women was done for the night and she left his side for the comfort of their bedroom. Herod sat torpidly making no sound except for the occasional belch from his excesses with food and drink. With Herodias now absent, Herod spoke of his regret and disappointment with his wife.

"What do you think of my wife?" He inquired of Pilate.

Pilate searched for the correct response. "Your spouse becomes you and glorifies your court with her beauty."

Herod responded with a chuckle. "I see that you are not unfamiliar with the delicacies of proper manner. This explains how you have come so easily to your present status in Judea. Did you persuade Emperor Tiberius with the same guile and finesse?"

"I influence Tiberius by what he wants most, my success in triumphant ventures that will broaden and enhance his domain, and glorify his name."

"My friend, you are far too modest. I find it difficult to trust anyone who does not fully reveal their pride over their achievements."

"I find it dangerous to take too much pride in those efforts that are dedicated to the Emperor, lest he becomes known for greater ambitious inclinations."

Herod laughed with a sigh of relief. "I like you, Pilate. Your loyalty to Tiberius precedes you and loyalty is a rare commodity in these troubled times. The Emperor has chosen you wisely for this charge."

"Forgive my impudent question, but why are you so fearful for your throne? As I understand, your rule is unquestioned since the Emperor Augustus validated your father's will that you are heir to this part of Judea."

"You have no idea how unruly family can become when familial love is pushed aside for the sake of a throne. My brothers, like myself, wanted to be king of Judea, but my father granted his throne to me in his second will."

"A second will?" asked Pilate.

"Yes. Aristobulus and Alexander, my older brothers from his marriage to Mariamme, were his first choices. Father changed the will after they were executed and my brother Antipater tried to poison him. I became first choice in his second will."

Pilate muttered under his breath, "I am beginning to understand."

"Father changed his mind again," said Herod. "I suspect he was swayed by another of his sons, Archelaus. Father always favored his word over mine. Herodias' family supported my plea to Augustus for absolute rule over all of Judea, but Augustus saw fit to ratify father's final will and divide the kingdom, leaving me with only Galilee and Perea. Archelaus had to also be content with not being king."

Pontius was silent before he spoke. "All is settled and you have nothing to fear. If you are afraid of Rome, I assure you that Tiberius is quite content to leave you with your own troubles. He cares not about your kingdom, unless there is a revolt against Rome that he would have to contend with."

Herod began to fidget. "There is one problem."

"And that would be?"

Herod let his eyes glaze in thought. "The stargazers told me that a first born within my kingdom would become known as King of the Jews. I sent out my armies to slay every first born son before this came to pass."

"I am not moved by the words of astrologers. Many have been driven mad by the desert sun and cannot be trusted. In any case, did you find the child and eliminate him?"

"A king cannot afford the luxury to ignore such a warning. Many kingdoms have been lost because of such heavenly elucidations. There were many slain, but..."

"But what?"

"I cannot be sure that I have killed him. I am haunted by dreams that leave me trembling because he is still coming. That was thirty years ago. If he lives, he is a man now and I have cause to fear him."

"Rest assured he is dead and you only have your nightmares to haunt you."

"Everyday there is another prophet, another messiah rising up to declare his importance. I am comforted to know that they do not move the people and of no consequence."

Pilate stood up. "King Herod, as Procurator and Governor of all Judea, it is my duty to keep the peace. This includes making you secure within your kingdom. Your enemies are my enemies. I shall make these misfits feel the might and the power of Rome.

"I shall round them up like cattle. I will crush them and their hopes. I shall find grievous fault with their talk and imprison every one that threatens the peace. The dangerous ones will be executed."

Herod looked at Pilate with fondness. "Since you are in a mood to serve me as well as Rome, you can investigate the one they call John the Baptist. He immerses his followers in the River Jordan and speaks of a prophet who is mightier than himself and comes with fire. That disturbs me. Bring John to me. I wish to speak with this man."

Pilate brought his right arm against his breastplate. "He who is against you is against Rome. I shall make this John my captive."

At midmorning, Pilate set out from Jerusalem with thirty centurions on horseback and afoot to find John the Baptist. This assignment was not difficult. John spoke openly among the crowds and many knew where he stayed. His popularity was apparent. Pilate took no chance that John had supporters ready to defend him. After two days' ride to Cyprus where he set up camp, Pilate led his men on a half day's journey to the River Jordan where John's last location was reported.

Pilate treated the excursion as he would any campaign. He followed military procedure and created a perimeter stockade where they encamped. Though he did not expect the Baptist to surprise his troops with an assault, he intended to be careful.

When the troops arrived at the river, all was tranquil. Pilate perceived no immediate danger and ordered his troops to relieve themselves of the heat by entering the water. Pilate dismounted his horse, Ares, and removed his helmet, wiping the sweat from his brow. He could see up the river to its bend. A group of people stood in the water, singing and clapping along with the musicians playing on the bank.

His military experience led him to count the

numbers and strengths of his possible foes along with noting their locations. He divided the centurions to flank John on both banks to stop him from fleeing his captors.

John was uninterested in the Roman soldiers amassing along the river. He submerged his followers one after the other and proclaimed so that all nearby could hear, "I baptize you in the name of the Holy Spirit, but one will come after me and baptize you with fire! Rise now, washed and cleansed spirit, in readiness for the redemption of our Lord and Savior."

Pilate sat quietly on Ares and listened. He leaned over the saddle to stretch his legs. He held the reins loosely while he waited for the right moment to descend upon John.

The governor led his horse into the shallows while John worked with his devotees. When Pilate was nearly on top of him, John turned and faced him without flinching. "I have baptized two centurions this week. If you are ready, prepare yourself. You will need to dismount from your horse."

"I am not here to bathe, Baptist. I must say you do have more nerve than I expected. Do you know to whom you speak?"

John pulled wet hair from of his face. "I suspect you will tell me when you are ready."

"I am Pilate, Governor of Judea, and I am here to

arrest you, Baptist."

"On what offense?" he asked.

"I could say 'because I feel like it,' but you are gathered unlawfully and have offended your king. You have offended Rome as well."

"That lascivious adulterer who sleeps with his brother's wife still calls himself king? He leads his people in darkness and flaunts his sin before the eyes of God. I will not yield. He is not my king. The real king is yet to come."

Pilate moved Ares closer. John stood his ground. "We are peaceful. These people have come to worship God and there is no law against peaceful worship."

"Perhaps so," Pilate said, "but we have come for you, Baptist. And who is this king you speak of?"

John did not answer.

"Your words are seditious and full of rebellion. If you do not answer to King Herod, you will answer to me."

Pilate called to his men while he turned Ares toward the other riverbank. "Put him in chains." The horse reared on his hind legs as Pilate commanded, "And scatter the rest of these pitiful people. They disgust me."

***

The centurions and their prisoner arrived back in Jerusalem by nightfall on the third day. Pilate dismounted his horse and stroked Ares' neck. He sought out the keeper.

"Feed and water him well, and brush him down. He deserves the attention, don't you, boy?"

Ares whinnied and snorted.

"Yes, Governor," said the keeper. "Right away."

Pilate pointed to the palace servant coming down the steps. "You! Tell the king that Pilate has brought an end to his nightmares."

He turned to the centurions. "Do not imprison John just yet. Remove the neck brace and leave him in chains to bring before Herod. He will want to speak with him."

King Herod sat on the throne with Herodias to his left. Pilate announced his own arrival as he entered, and brought his arm against his breastplate in salute. "King Herod, I apologize if I have disturbed you, but I thought you would want to see the Baptist."

Herod raised his hand clutching a silken cloth and waved Pilate on in response to his salute. "You need not worry. Dispense with the pleasantries. So this is the prophet I've been hearing so much about."

John stood in front of Herod. Only the sound of his chains rattling against each other spoke for him. He was haggard and weak from the long march to the city.

His body was bronzed from the sun and his hair matted like hemp. Herod asked him to give some sense of salutation, and he could hardly lift his chains. John dropped to one knee, not because he wanted to honor Herod, but because he could no longer stand.

His words were parched from the trek across the desert. "I have thirst."

"Did you hear that, Pilate?" said Herod. "The man is in need of drink. A man who spends his time at the river should have no thirst at all."

He lunged from his throne and approached John, encircling him for a better view. Herod lifted John's head by the chin and looked into his reddened eyes, and shoved him away with disgust. Calling for a servant to bring water, he took the ladle and splashed John in the face. "There," he said with satisfaction. "I was told you had much to say about me and my wife. So prophet, tell me now."

John mustered what little strength he had. "The Holy Spirit beckons me to speak. Repent, oh sinner of the ages. You are an abomination. You cast off your real wife as old clothing, then soil your bed with your lust for your brother's wife, little more than a concubine on display for a sinister plan of political deceit. You have made her a whore's whore, a harlot bride in silken raiment. You bring darkness upon this house, a palace of ill repute and wickedness, a place of regal squalor."

Herod struck him across the face and knocked him down. "Silence, you pitiful desert viper. Do you think you can talk in my court with such disrespect to your king and queen?

Herodias spoke to her king. "How can you let him live? Kill this miserable excuse of a man. He calls himself a prophet and uses his station to chastise you, to spout and spread foul pronouncements. This John is evil to malign us, especially me. He is a malignant bastard, a false prophet. Better that he should be drawn and quartered in the square for all to see, or better yet, thrown in the dungeon and eaten by rats."

As the queen stole his anger and replaced it with her own, King Herod used the moment to think. To carry out such punishments would be unwise and perhaps even dangerous, he thought. A just cause had to be established before he slew the popular prophet.

Herodias screamed at Herod. "Kill him now, or are you afraid?"

Herod raised his hand. "Oh no my dear Herodias, we must not be too quick with our vengeance. We must think these actions through carefully. Killing a prophet is one thing, but this John might mean more trouble for us and have grave and far-reaching consequences for civil unrest.

"Pilate, take this wretched creature away. Put him

in the dungeon for now until we can consider what to do with him."

"By your command," responded Pilate.

Revolt in the Streets

Pontius Pilate returned to his quarters, enraged and helpless. Given the chance, he would not have spared John. He was especially intolerant of disobedience and insubordination. The Baptist's outburst toward King Herod made Pilate seethe with anger.

He outstretched his hand to see it shake. Pilate grabbed his sword from its sheath and clenched the grip. He pulled the blade into his fingers while his hand remained shaking. Turning the sword from edge to edge and aligning it with his arm, he followed the sword's edge toward the tip until his fingers bled. Blood dripped along the blade until the shaking stopped. The idea was not to mind the pain but to greet it. He always did this before a battle to calm himself.

The appearance of the Baptist had ominous implications. His disregard for Herod's authority, together with the show of his attitude at the river, revealed an awful portent of doom. The Baptist, Pilate realized, could be the center of a serious plot to incite rebellion against Herod, and later Rome itself. This thought caused Pilate's anger to escalate against the self-proclaimed prophets and spiritual misfits roaming the streets of Jerusalem. He wanted to round them up for a wholesale slaughter. A swift Roman justice was necessary, he thought, neat and quick.

He smiled at himself and grunted with satisfaction at the recognition of his position. "I'm surprised at you," he murmured. "Why do you behave like a frightened old woman?" He remembered the symbol of Roman power he still held. Pilate wiped the blood on his tunic with silent pride, and sheathed the sword, and his thoughts continued. *It will be like crushing ants on a hill.*

He pushed aside his concern for political finesse in favor of his military experience. The soldier in him promised to replace his hesitation with expedience. He called to his manservants for wine. One servant removed his breastplate and tunic, while the other held out his robe and wine.

"Prepare my bath," he said. "I will collect my thoughts while I soak."

Pilate knew he needed to resolve this issue quickly. He was determined to increase the recognition of power. Not the weakness of Herod's power, but the real power that was Rome. Gulping wine from his cup, he complained, "My bath water is cold. Shall I freeze in my own quarters? Bring more hot water."

The servants bowed their heads and scurried out of

the room. Pilate sat with his feet submerged in the water, determined to find ways he could impress greater force upon the populace. Wrapped in his robes, he called for his favorite tribune to come to his quarters.

Marcellus Septimus arrived out of breath, with his leather tunic lashed over one shoulder. He found Pilate standing over charts and maps as if he were planning battle strategy.

"By the gods, forgive me for the delay. Is this a matter of great urgency?" said Septimus.

Pilate responded kindly. "Forgive me for awakening you at this hour, but I felt troubled by what I have seen this day. We are infested by a troublesome plague that would infiltrate the underbelly of Rome."

Septimus stiffened. "Are we under siege from the armies along the border of Nubitia? I have heard rumors they have sent raids to probe the strength of our forces."

Pilate smiled at the young tribune. "No, my friend, it is worse than that. The problem is within these walls, within this city. The reluctance to act permeates the palace and we must act before we find ourselves, our women, and our children with their throats cut before the passing of the night.

"I want to catch this treachery. Now here is my plan. In the morning, gather the metal smiths and take a centurion to every hovel and collect all of the coins you can. Make sure you keep an accounting. We don't want them thinking their occupiers are also thieves. I want you to make a public proclamation that all coinage will be worthless unless it bears the image of the Emperor. Is that understood?"

"Yes, Governor."

"Oh, and place on every street corner a standard with Tiberius' image raised high, to remind them who is the emperor in this city."

"The people will be upset. What about the Great Temple?"

"Especially around the temple. Now go."

Septimus slapped his tunic with obedience. "By your leave, Governor."

**

In the afternoon of the following day, crowds gathered in front of the Temple with outcries of injustice. Small groups grumbled about the standards and collected in front of the palace to voice their complaints to King Herod. "We demand recognition of our rights as citizens. What of our coins? Give us our money back."

Protests were heard from the temple. "What will become of our offerings? Romans are defiling our money. This is sacrilege. They defile the temple with their graven images of the Emperor."

Soldiers surrounded the mob from above the walls and aimed their spears down in readiness to kill the outspoken. A stone was cast and struck a soldier before he could raise his shield. He fell to his knees. This was followed by a shower of rocks that bounced off a wall of shields. Spears rained down on the crowd. A rock thrower was struck in the leg and another through the chest. The soldiers laughed at the wounded and cheered each other's marksmanship. Praetorians on horseback brought their horses into those still standing to disperse them, but the crowd resisted. A horseman called out, "Guards, arrest these rebels."

The Praetorian forced his horse to trample on those close by and yelled over their cries, "Get back, you swine."

A man struggled to get free from the two centurions. "What is the charge? We have done nothing wrong?"

"For disorderly conduct," said the Praetorian. "And for speaking against the Emperor!"

Soldiers formed a ring around those left standing among the pools of spilled blood. Their hands were bound and they were linked together by more rope before being led away. One horseman dismounted and tied a rope around the feet of the gathered dead. He tied the rope to his saddle, remounted, and pulled on his horse to drag the limp carcasses. The bodies bobbed as they were pulled over the rugged cobblestones, washing them with their blood. Onlookers turned away and went back to their homes.

***

Later that evening, the priests Josephus and Nicodemus appeared at the entrance to the Great Temple. The last rays of sunlight shone through clouds of dust and the early evening wind gusted against their long white robes, sweeping them away from their inner beige garibias. Each wore a wide cobalt blue sash draped along one side and tucked under his belt.

Matching blue hats sat tall on their heads, making them appear stately. The hats had rounded but narrow bottoms and flattened at the top. White panels draped to the shoulders and flapped in the breeze to expose long curls of black hair. Their beards were salt and pepper gray, and woven into stiffened squares that gave a chiseled look to their boney features.

The priests' coal-black eyes stared at the faces of the crowd. The people moved closer and their grumbling ceased as the priests signaled for quiet.

Nicodemus spoke first. "Friends, calm yourselves.

There is no reason to be alarmed. The Romans mean you no harm, and you must not resist or there be more bloodshed."

A merchant stepped on the staircase that led to the temple platform. "They have taken away our money. When shall we be repaid?"

Josephus raised his hand against the tumult. "Be not afraid. We have been assured that your money will be returned."

Another merchant spoke. "But what will happen now that our money has been defiled by the Emperor's image? What shall we do about the law? How shall we bring offerings to the temple?"

"Hear me dear ones," said Nicodemus. "We have spoken to the High Priest Caiaphas. He is making preparations within the temple to exchange your money for shekels. Use these for your offerings without fear of angering God in His house of prayer."

The people turned to each other in discussion as the priests retreated into the temple, confident they had turned the tide of unrest. The temporary measure of exchanging the new coins for shekels did not appease the zealots. They were not easy to persuade and zealots needed little reason to complain. Besides the coins, the appearance of Roman standards in front of the Great Temple was an outrage and more than enough cause for the zealots to rise up with violence.

The priests used them to voice their own complaints without taking on the wrath of Rome, and the Sanhedrin often hid behind the zealots bad behavior with the same tactic.

Within the Great Temple walls was another tempest. The priests struggled to deal with reports of new messiahs, as foretold by the old prophets, and one or another appeared almost every day. They did not resist the idea of a messiah, but wanted to ascertain if they were genuine to consider seriously, or discard them as blasphemers and a waste of their time.

Voices in the inner chambers echoed outside the inner-sanctum containing the holy of holies. The rooms interleaved as a great maze of concentric elongated chambers. Massive stones defined walls that rose to support the huge lintels strung overhead, and gave the appearance of a darkened cave. Shafts of dim light from the moon above the horizon shone through openings interspersed within the lintels, and layers of pungent incense containing frankincense and myrrh softened the vast areas of darkness. To an outsider the odorous effect seared the nostrils and invoked the need to choke. The priests were used to the smell and the closeness it created. They welcomed this minor suffering as the price paid for intimacy with God.

High Priest Caiaphas sat beneath one of the shafts

of light, to view those sitting nearby. His seat was elevated higher than the rest of the chamber. Gold and pale-blue light shone down around him. The flicker of oil lamps danced on his face. Though his robes were similar to the other priests, his sashes were made of purple and yellow silk.

Caiaphas spoke and the room became quiet. His words reverberated through the chamber like thunderclaps above the conversations, and fell on the priests like cool rain. They took their places on stone benches while others stood arguing passionately. Caiaphas played with his beard while he listened, uppermost in his mind the responsibility to guide his flock with prudence. It was reminiscent of the Senate of Rome.

The priests reported of deeds done by prophets, or inspired words from this one or that as possible signs of a chosen one. They entered into arguments about the content of the words along with their meaning and implications. Others continued to argue in fear about the possible derision of the law.

Jeremiah lashed out against the self-proclaimed harbingers of change. "Who are these wretched devils that we should give an ear to their babble? They emerge from the desert, as if the sun and desert gives them their authority. Should we let them speak because of their long-suffering? Their ideas of reform are bound within a new interpretation of old teachings. All they really want is to carelessly change what has been divinely given to us by our God for their own ends."

The priests shared the belief and fear, mixed with excitement and hope, of the one that might come. For Caiaphas, these prophets disguised themselves as visionaries and sought to alter the law. They did not revere the law and wanted to tear it down.

"These revisionists are heretics and blasphemers," declared Caiaphas. "We have seen them come and go before. This is no different. My brothers, do not let these beggars and thieves turn you from the truth. The law is clear. We need the law, we love the law, and God gave it to us with love through his shepherd Moses. The priesthood needs to watch over and protect his flock from these misguided wrong doers. It is our task to make sure that the law is not defiled or abated."

Joseph stepped forward with concern. "Master Caiaphas, how are we to know the chosen one if we discard any of those that come?"

Caiaphas placed his hand upon Joseph's shoulder. "Brother Joseph. I know you well. I have known your father and your brothers. Most of all, I know your heart. Do you think we would actually turn away the true Messiah? How would I know for sure?" Joseph looked at Caiaphas in anticipation of his answer. "The law lives inside me, it is my life. I will recognize and know him because the law will live inside him too. By his arrival, he will fulfill the law. I will know him because it will flow from him like a river, and all the prophets will sing his praises."

He turned toward the other priests and continued. "I tell you this day that when he comes, and he will come, by the words of the holy prophets, we will greet him with open arms and loving hearts and truly rejoice in his coming. It will mean that God will live on the earth again and we will have prepared the way, my brothers."

The priests gathered around Caiaphas, pleased and comforted by his words of encouragement. He added, "Go, my brothers, and greet our flock with kindness and compassion for their wants and needs. Do not be afraid to offer stern reminders that the Pharisees represent the way and the light like our fathers before us, and ensure that these devils are quickly forgotten."

The Nazarene Returns

Every season this year has been more hot and dry than usual. Rumors of the promised messiah fill the streets of Jerusalem like a flash flood during the spring rains. Prophets descended from everywhere. They emerge faster than bread baked in the street ovens during festivals. Each is more crazed than the next, crawling out of dung holes and dirty street corners. They claim the right to be the one called from the one true god, whatever that means. For me, I only know the gods of Rome, the ones I grew up with, and my one true god, Rome itself.

I have heard of this man, Jeshua the Nazarene. Some zealots are frightened at the mention of his name, while others turn teary-eyed when he is spoken of in conversation. I find this to be disturbing. He had not even arrived in Jerusalem and his reputation precedes him.

Reports of his return come from Tyre. A trader returning from Samaria brought news of him. It is said this Nazarene can perform miracles. This upsets me.

***

Jeshua descended the mountains during the middle of the Vernal Equinox. Joses and Simon, Jeshua's brothers, waited for him on the slopes of Mount Tabor. His return was a high point for his family. They have waited for more than a week.

The wind gusted, carrying with it the sweet smell of jasmine flowers. Weather was unpredictable at this time of the year, and Jeshua had to delay sailing to Judea for three weeks. Once in Judea, he traveled three hard days from the port of Tyre on foot with a donkey in tow.

Anxious to meet their brother after many years, Simon and Joses had only stories of him told by others. Passing caravans that bore magi out of the East carried his exploits. Since their childhood in Nazareth, young Joses and Simon believed Jeshua to be a legend or myth. He was only a boy of twelve when he left, and his return took more than 22 years. Jeshua was rumored to have trained in the East, and the elders never spoke of this in public. The brothers expected to greet a man, and a stranger. Simon and Joses argued during their long wait whether they would recognize him.

They formed many questions and disagreed about who would be the first to ask. Simon being older was eager to hear what Jeshua had studied in the East. Joses wanted to know about the foreign lands. There would be time to talk when they arrived at home, where there was much longing to see him again.

The brothers fancied the celebration of his homecoming. There would be a great feast, they ventured. Simon laughed as he imagined the wine he would drink, the fresh fruit he would eat, and the olive oil for his bread. He imagined the fondness of good company and seeing his friends and family. Joses laughed aloud because the warmth of family was what he missed the most.

The hot, dry wind parched Simon's lips and made it difficult to chew the morsel of flatbread he brought along for the journey. It reminded him of the unreality of their fantasies. His thoughts turned to his father's words to mind after Joses. They had little food and their water-skins hung loosely over their donkeys, reserved for drinking only. The brothers were strangers and not welcome, as the people were suspicious by nature. Locals guarded the well water and not eager to share it.

Simon and Joses sat high on a hill overlooking the ravine that sloped from the mountains further away. This was the most likely path from the port of Tyre. The donkeys were tied near an olive tree and left to graze protected from the hot sun. They propped riding sticks under a blanket and pulled it over them like a common cloak, to sit huddled together and wait for the afternoon tide. Morning tide had come and gone, and no one passed that fit Jeshua's description. Soon they fell asleep, one lumped over the other like bags of figs.

A cool breeze signaled the wane of the sun. Soon it became considerably colder. The drop in temperature awakened Simon. He rubbed his eyes to find a donkey standing free in front of him. Simon took his riding stick and whacked Joses across his behind.

"Get off me you poor excuse of a brother," Simon scowled. "You have fallen asleep and now our donkeys are loose."

Joses rolled face down into the dust. He groaned and rubbed his belly. "Simon, I'm hungry. Have you any more bread?"

"All you can think of is food. If we lose the donkeys, you will be served for dinner when we get back. Now get off me and on your feet. We have to catch them. Be quick about it."

Laughter rolled from the outcropping of rocks above. The brothers stared through the evening light to locate and pinpoint the source. They made out not more than a mere shadow. The setting sun offered only a blinding red glare on the rock face. Alarm filled their hearts. The mocking had the high ground, leaving them vulnerable to attack.

Being younger, Joses was more apt to act impetuously. He held out his stick in front of himself in a threatening manner. Simon looked at his brother incredulously. "What are you going to do, little brother?"

Joses ignored him. "I warn you thief, we are not unaccustomed to engaging in violence."

The laughter changed to a roar as the shadow dropped from above and startled them. The sudden movement made them jump back. Then the shadow spoke. His voice broke melodic and soft on the breeze blowing against them.

"You certainly have heart, I'll give you that. I am pleased to have such fine young men escort me to Nazareth. I am already experiencing safety," he said chuckling. "You need not concern yourself about your donkeys. The one wandering about is mine. He has carried the burdensome yoke of my wares long enough. The animal deserves to rest for a time and graze anywhere he chooses, especially after such a long journey from Tyre."

Joses and Simon met Jeshua's eyes and they dropped to their knees. His eyes were black, but burned like golden embers.

"Master," said Simon. "We are sorry to have kept you waiting."

"On the contrary, my brothers. I have kept you."

The three gathered their belongings and made their way down the mountain. Joses still complained of having hunger pains. Jeshua stopped for a moment. "I sense your deeper feelings and it is not your hunger that I feel, but desperation."

Jeshua placed his hand on Joses' shoulder. "You believe you will not find your way in life without being in the shadow of your elder brother. You believe that life will pass you by while you are forgotten among your brothers and sisters.

"Simon was annoyed. "Put away the petty need to fill your belly for once. Our master is tired from his journey and needs to be free of your demands. I have no more bread, so you will have to wait."

Jeshua raised his hand toward Simon. "Brother Simon, will you be a party to your brother's desperation? Have compassion for his pain. The world bears the pain and agony, enough for everyone, you do not need to add to it."

Simon bowed his head and Joses felt ashamed for asking for more. He withdrew with tears in his eyes. He said with anger, "I will be happy to carry my need quietly. I will bother no one any further."

Jeshua pressed his hand against his younger brother's heart. "Joses, how is it possible that you cannot know that everything is there for you at your command? Never be afraid to ask for what you want. Reach into your sack and take your fill. Our journey is not over, it has just begun."

Joses reached into his bag and found fresh bread to eat and fruit as well. He took a handful of dates and tore off a piece of bread from a full loaf while displaying them happily to Simon. With tears in his eyes and bread stuck between his teeth, Joses handed a piece to Simon. "Here brother, I have plenty and can give to you for a change."

Simon took the bread from his brother and turned to Jeshua, quite puzzled. He faced the road ahead and began to walk.

They walked without talking until the darkness had overtaken them. Only the stars lighted their way. Jeshua felt the need to rest. He beckoned them to make camp and build a fire to ward off the desert cold for the night. Simon and Joses bedded down and quickly fell to sleep as the fire crackled.

Jeshua lay awake. The trouble between his brothers provided an insight into the deeper agony that existed within the hearts of many people. As he meditated on this, sadness brought him to tears. How he might change the world with what he learned from his masters in the East? That question plagued him throughout his training and his masters did not provide the answer.

The old feeling came over him, the same he had from earliest childhood that gnawed at his spirit and drew him into a sense of his fate. It ended with the same conclusion. His purpose was to return to the world and change the heart of humanity, a daunting task that left him very much alone. He looked up at the stars and wondered where this would all end.

Jeshua closed his eyes, bowed his head, and fell into prayer. He asked for help in the coming time until fear wiggled through his thoughts. Doubt crept in as he viewed his thoughts. Everyone said he was the chosen one. For a moment, he questioned the idea. In his weakness, light surrounded him and interrupted his doubt.

He opened his eyes to see a field of light take form. The light coalesced until he saw a tall figure in front of him, an angel. A delicate sound grew into a piercing shriek and called out his name.

The angel said, "Jeshua, fear not! The hour is at hand for your unfolding."

Jeshua had seen spirits before, even as a child, but they rarely spoke. "Why are you here, spirit? Who is it that interrupts my prayer?"

"I am Melchizedek and have come here to impart the power and authority to act on behalf of the One who shall remain nameless. You shall inherit His Will and pass this on to all of humanity, a message of love, compassion, and hope. You will come to know this Will as the force of the Christ."

Jeshua knelt and wept as Melchizedek continued.

"This charge is yours to carry for three Earth years. I will come again to take this charge from you. During this time, you will be known as the Christ and prepare those you choose to follow and embody the nameless One's Will, so that all can know and understand the truth."

The angel pressed his hand against Jeshua's head, and fire burned inside and spread through his body. The intensity grew and he collapsed. Jeshua whimpered to the angel, "Who is the nameless One that calls on me?"

Melchizedek started to dissolve. "He is your Father, who rules everything in this reality and brings freedom."

The angel faded and left only the shining stars. Jeshua fell into deep sleep.

Morning sun gripped the dunes that lay to the East with gentle fingers. The light fell on the travelers as a warm and comforting blanket, which loosened the desert night's cold chill, and awakened them. Simon opened his eyes and yawned into a deep stretch. Joses awoke next and they both turned to Jeshua.

"Master," Simon called out. "Are you awake?"

Jeshua did not answer.

The Blind and the Dead

To be procurator of the most difficult province in Judea, one has to be practical and prudent as well. It is wise to be cautious when the appearance of miracles is afoot. These are strange days and I must keep my own counsel, if for no other reason than to hold my reason under a tight leash.

The problem of lunatic prophets running amuck in the streets raising doubt and fear in the people makes for interesting and difficult management, but when the events turn to supernatural occurrences, then I have to take a step back and wonder how I shall manage this.

I am above all a sensible Roman soldier. Some might say that I am a superb leader of men. I have fought many battles in my time against formidable foes, even outnumbered on a few occasions. But never have I had to deal with forces beyond my capacity to handle with certainty.

This man Jeshua is an enigma. He plagues my mind with great uncertainty and I have not yet met this man... this prophet man. To me, he is only another lunatic giving promises to the poor and wretched, desperate to be free of their burden. He is another deceiver weaving a web of hope for the hopeless. I wonder why he stands above the rest of the misfits.

The desert eventually has its way with weary men. Sand storms rise without warning, and the desert conjures from its hot and dusty depths a foul and savage creature to sway the mind into madness and drag its host into an untimely death.

Often have I chuckled to myself in a late evening stupor from the endless reservoir of wine spilling from my cup, that nothing good can come out of the desert. It was one of those private evenings when the wine had a flavor of sweet retreat that news of this prophet entered my sanctuary. As procurator, I had to pay attention.

***

The centurion entered with the sound of leather clashing against Roman armor. His clenched fist struck his breastplate, and he announced his presence. "Your pardon, I bring an urgent message."

Pilate groaned. "At this late hour?"

"Many apologies, Governor. A man stumbled into our encampment in hysterics, laughing one moment and breaking down to sob in the next. At first we thought he was just another rebel causing trouble. In his clamoring, the man kept proclaiming, 'It's a miracle, it's a miracle.'

"He seemed delirious, and appeared exhausted and dehydrated. The man had walked the desert until he came on to us. One of my men gave him water. He calmed a little, but kept babbling about a young rabbi that came into his village the night before. The rabbi preached a little, but then took notice of the man's son, who had been blind since birth. This rabbi said, 'I shall prove that even if blind, one can still see the truth.' He took a water-skin and poured water into his hands and let it fall to the ground. The rabbi scooped up the mud and bathed his son's face. He told the boy to go wash. Afterward, his son declared that he could see.

"We asked the old man where this took place. He described the village of Gabaon, not half a day's ride far from our camp. We found the village and sought out the man's son. He could clearly see us. He was overjoyed that we had recovered his father from the desert. The other villagers confirmed the man's story that his son was blind since birth and now could see."

Pilate's brow became deeply furrowed. "What did you find out about this rabbi? Did you get a name?"

The centurion tightened his lips and grit his teeth. "We asked about the rabbi. They said his name was Jeshua. We scouted the area and could not find a trace of him. Despite our threats to the villagers not to hide him from us, we still could not find the rabbi."

Pilate set down his cup of wine. He ran his hand through his hair and straightened his tunic. "Very well. You have done a day's work, centurion. Before you return to your troops, take what you need from my stores and distribute it among your men."

The centurion saluted once again and was about to leave when Pilate stopped him. "Keep your eyes and ears open for more of this rabbi Jeshua. I will expect a full report on your next discovery. And, if you find him, bring him to me."

***

Jeshua had left in the middle of the night, though his bedding remained and his belongings hung on the donkey. The brothers did not know whether to wait or continue on their journey. Simon pushed back his disappointment and stirred the sand despondently with his riding stick. He was confused by Jeshua's leaving. He could not understand why he did not tell them where he was going. Simon had counted on their returning together.

Joses was not concerned about what happened to Jeshua. He wanted to leave before the sun rose too high. Simon insisted they wait for Jeshua's return. By the time the sun was overhead, Simon conceded that Jeshua was not coming. Joses told his brother that

Jeshua would probably meet them later, and helped pack their goods. After all, Jeshua did entrust them with his belongings and this proved he would join them.

Simon concluded that Jeshua must have had pressing business elsewhere and did not have time to tell them of his plans. In any case, he still held out hope that Jeshua would meet with them along the road before they returned home. They were not far from Ephraim, a village located a half a day further south. There, Simon believed, they would have news of Jeshua. By evening, the concern was to find a place to bed down and find something to eat. They were closer to home and finding suitable lodging was less difficult. The people in Ephriam were more friendly and hospitable to Nazarenes than the inhabitants of Tyre. Simon and Joses inquired with several innkeepers about Jeshua's passing, but none had seen him. Simon negotiated for lodging and meals for the night. He and his brother fell fast asleep with the intent to make an early start.

At first light, Simon was checking the tightness of the cinches on the donkeys while his brother slept. Jeshua appeared. "Did you sleep well, my brothers?"

Joses rose, still half asleep. "Well enough."

"Thank you for taking care of my things in my absence. I was called away on my Father's business and did not want to wake you."

Simon was puzzled. "Our father has not seen you in many years, master. How could you have business with him when we have yet to arrive home?"

"I do not speak of your father, but of my Father in heaven. Do not trouble yourself by this, my brother. One day you shall understand with greater measure. I promise."

The brothers emerged from the inn to find themselves surrounded by soldiers on horseback.

Octavius, the leader, adjusted himself in his saddle. He leaned back and counted his men to measure his strength against a possible foe. He slowly turned to gaze at the trio in front of him.

His helmet and breastplate armor gleamed in the midday sun, and offered a sharp contrast to the red bristled plumage that jutted from his helmet. The drape of his red cape fell from his shoulders against his horse, soaking up the sweat and dust gathered from a long ride. He stared down at Jeshua. "Are you the one they call Jeshua, the rabbi?"

Jeshua took a step forward and Octavius' horse backed away. "Yes. I am he, son of Joseph the Essene."

"The procurator of Judea wants to question you. You must come with us to Jerusalem," commanded Octavius.

Simon stepped in front of Jeshua. "What business

do you have with my brother? He has done nothing wrong."

The soldiers closed in on the boy, and pressed against him with the might of their horses.

Jeshua pulled Simon back. "Fear not, little brother. There is no harm in talk. Go to your father and tell him I will be home shortly. This is but a slight delay. Do not worry."

***

Jeshua traveled two days with the soldiers before they reached Bethany. The day before, Martha had learned of Jeshua's healing of the blind boy in Gabaon and sent word for him that Lazareth was ill and close to death. Jeshua already knew of Lazareth's illness, and planned to make him part of his ministry.

The soldiers stopped to water the horses from the well at the village square when a messenger approached Jeshua.

"Master," he pleaded, "you must come. Lazareth is near dying and only you can save him."

"My friend, you are too late. Lazareth has already entered into the sleep," said Jeshua.

The messenger was puzzled by the remark. "But master, how could this be?"

Jeshua lifted his head. "Do not lament for

Lazareth. Death does not mean an end to life but simply a transition. Though he has entered sleep, he will arise. His awakening will prove to those with eyes to see and ears to hear that my Father takes the sting of death away and brings assurance for an everlasting life."

He walked with the messenger toward Martha's dwelling. Lacusius, a Roman soldier, approached the rabbi. Jeshua raised his hand and fell the soldier to his knees and he could not get up.

"Will you resist the will of my Father, who gives life and can also take it away?" asked Jeshua.

The other horsemen were stunned and came quickly to the aid of Lacusius on the ground. As they tended to him, Jeshua entered into the house of Martha. He bid hello to Martha, who was at the foot of Lazaerth's bed and weeping for the loss of his life.

She turned to Jeshua. "Master, if only you could have come sooner. I am afraid that you are too late to save him. He is gone."

"My dear Martha, do not lament. The hour is at hand to raise him up and demonstrate a great truth. Leave me so I can tend to him."

Martha stopped crying and Jeshua attended to Lazareth. He pulled back the curtain surrounding the bed and sat beside the dead body of Lazareth. "I am here Father. Blessed be your way. Let your continence shine down upon this man. Let the life that lives within you live within him once again. Jod He Vau He Amain."

Jeshua took a deep breath and a bright light shown about him and Lazareth's body. He let out his breath in a long slow sigh. "Parsham...cayham...beheh...meheh she-uud."

Jeshua shoved his thumb deep into Lazareth's groin. "Lazareth," he declared, "Come forth and awaken."

The dead man shook with a jolt and opened his eyes.

Jeshua appeared in the doorway with Lazareth standing next to him and looking confused. Martha and her sister Mary fell to their knees and kissed Jeshua's feet with great joy and flowing tears. "O Sanna, Hey Sanna, blessed be, blessed be. The Messiah has come. The Messiah has come."

Martha looked at Jeshua's face as it shown brighter than the sunlight. He said, "Your faith and the will of my Father have spoken today. Behold, your Lazareth brings to the world proof of everlasting life. Go tell the people what you have seen today."

Jeshua left the village to rejoin Simon and Joses in Ephriam. The Roman soldiers made no effort to stop him. Octavius held Lacusius, who attempted to get to his feet. Jeshua turned his gaze toward them. "Do not worry, his weakness will pass. I meant him no permanent harm. The strength will return to his legs soon enough." He continued past the well and the village square. The soldiers mounted their horses and had no wish to engage with Jeshua again.

Octavius lamented having to return to Jerusalem without his prisoner. He would have to report the events that unfolded in Bethany. Pilate would not be happy about his returning without Jeshua, or that the rabbi had brought down a Roman soldier with the wave of his hand.

"Prophets are men in rags and can be easily dealt with. A strong Roman arm that skillfully wields a sharp sword is a power like no other in Judea. But what use is a sword against this? This is magic, the work of a sorcerer," said Octavius.

Jeshua's power frightened Octavius. If he could fell one soldier, then he could do the same to one hundred. How does the sword stand against that kind of power? Octavius turned to the other soldiers.

"This rabbi is a threat to Rome itself. Come quickly. We must hasten to Jerusalem. Pilate needs to know we are facing a threat from a new and dangerous enemy."

The soldiers rode out in a roar of pounding hooves, leaving Jeshua far behind in a cloud of dust.

Caiaphas and the Counsel

Stories of Jeshua spread throughout Judea. His goings and comings had a disturbing effect on everyone, including the Sanhedrin. Change was afoot and no one accepted it lightly. Caiaphas, High Priest of the Counsel of the Sanhedrin, was no exception.

Caiaphas sat engrossed in scripture when he heard people arguing outside his chambers. He emerged to find several Pharisees having a heated discussion about a young rabbi. The primary issue was whether or not this young rabbi was actually the Messiah.

Some defended the rabbi, and others said the stories were only rumors and hearsay.

"Even so, this talk is blasphemy," said a Pharisee. They gasped when told that the rabbi had allegedly performed miracles in the north. The voices rose to a greater volume.

"What is this clamor about?" said Caiaphas. "Can't a brother study the scriptures quietly without all this noise?"

They bowed their heads with many apologies.

Nicodemus stepped forward. "Wonderful news has come from the north, Brother Caiaphas. A young rabbi has apparently restored the eyesight of a boy that had been blind from birth."

Caiaphas called for tea and stroked his beard. He always stroked his beard vigorously when he was agitated. He appeared disgruntled by Nicodemus' remarks. "Good news you say? One cannot cure such a condition. It is preposterous! If a man is blind at birth, it is God's will that he be so. Therefore, it is sacrilege to try to change it. What proofs have you, Brother Nicodemus?"

"Brother Caiaphas, we have yet to validate these reports, but I have sent Brother Levi to investigate. It may be a sign. I am keenly interested to meet and hear this man speak as well. They say he knows the scriptures by heart."

"My dear Nicodemus, we have been over this before. There have always been occurrences like these. Each time the promises and portents arise, we easily dispel them with simple explanations. You continue to chase after the signs like a young pupil. Yours is one of the brightest minds among us and your faith in the scriptures is admirable, but when will you give up this obsession and become more practical?"

Brother Joseph came forward. "Brother Caiaphas, I know of this one. I heard him speak when he was but a boy. Do you remember? He conversed freely at the temple for more than an hour to many of our brethren.

He answered our questions with great skill. It was quite astonishing. Could this be the same man? If so, then we need to examine this one more closely."

Caiaphas sipped his tea. "Yes, I remember now. The Nazarene boy, the one they called Jeshua. He was an oddity, a strange and obstinate lad. Was he not an Essene? If so, then this matter is of some consideration. The Essenes do not perceive the law as we do and might be troublesome."

"He was only 10 years old and that was more than 20 years ago," added Brother Nathaniel. "Surely, it cannot be the same boy. He was a freak of nature, an abomination in the eyes of the God."

"Brother Caiaphas, I can appreciate your candor and respect your opinion highly, yet, there is also something else," said Brother Nicodemus.

Caiaphas sipped on his tea and complained that it was too cold. He wanted to end this ridiculous banter over another misfit of the desert. He cleared his throat and the Counsel knew he was very upset. "Yes, Brother Nicodemus, what else have you to say?"

"There is also a rumor that he has returned a man from his death bed back to the living."

Nicodemus' words fell on the stone floor as though they were made with clinging metal, and echoed into the brother's ears.

"What did you say?" asked Caiaphas. "Consider

the weight of your speech before you let loose another word. We can forgive idle chatter from time to time, but this is of a very grave consequence."

"He has returned the dead to the living," said Nicodemus.

The brothers waited on Caiaphas' response.

"Blasphemy! I cannot believe my own ears at what you are saying. The power of life and death is reserved for the Most High God. To speak of any man, even a so-called prophet, in the same breath as the Father creator, that he could bring the dead back to life is nothing short of blasphemy! Nicodemus you have gone too far."

Nicodemus' eyes filled with tears. He pressed further. "Brother Caiaphas, I mean no disrespect. I only say that perhaps we have come to a time that has been prophesied in the scripture that the Lord God of our fathers would one day come forth and lead us into the new order. We cannot ignore these signs by self righteous indignation."

"Will you now add to your indiscretion and lecture your high priest on the understanding of the scripture?"

Nicodemus yielded. "By Your Grace, accept my humble apologies. I stand corrected before the Counsel."

Caiaphas knew that mercy is a great virtue and to

show mercy to Nicodemus would soften the blow in view of the others. At the same time, he had to maintain a tight reign over the Counsel. "Brother Nicodemus, many times you can be most impetuous and obstinate. Still, there is a measure of good judgment within you. Go with Levi to find this rabbi and observe him. Return in a fortnight with your evaluations."

"As you wish, Your Grace," answered Nicodemus.

The brothers smiled on Nicodemus and quietly cheered Caiaphas in his brilliant strategy of managing the conflict with minimal disturbance.

Nicodemus gathered what he would need for the journey to Gabaon, home to the blind man, and then later to Bethany, where Lazareth had been rescued.

Caiaphas confided to Jacob of his own plan. "We must be prudent in these matters and ensure that we have all of the facts. Go to the Nazarenes near the Sea of Galilee, and inquire at the home of Joseph and Mary as to the whereabouts of young Jeshua."

"Yes, Your Grace. I shall leave at once."

John Baptizes Jeshua

One aspect of public rule that is as consistent as the sun rising in the East is the intrigue, corruption, and struggle for power in the higher stations of rule. I never wanted any part of it.

Political life as a Republican in Rome was, at best, a roll of the dice. There are those who might also say that Roman rule, at any level, exists by honesty. I would declare such as fools, idealists at best, suited for the role of philosopher, record keeper, or scribe.

In Jerusalem, it is no different, except the interplay of intrigue enjoys a far better chance here than in Rome. With my station as Procurator of Judea, I can observe this in action without being too involved. That is the case with the prophet Jeshua.

The man who is the unfortunate pawn of this intrigue is the Baptist. Of course, I hold no high regard for those who roam the desert, misfits and troublemakers all of them. However, I admit that even as I hold no moral obligation to the Baptist, I do have a measure of compassion for his innocence in this matter.

As their overseer, I have observed the people of Judea. Their ritual of baptism is nothing but an excuse to dodge their daily tasks and a delightful way to avoid the heat. Their dedication to the Baptist is more about personal gratification than spirituality.

***

King Herod struggled with the problem of John the Baptist. His wife was infuriated by John's public insults toward their royal private life and she pressed the king to punish him. But the Baptist's popularity continued to grow with the people and served only to limit the king's choices.

Having John killed would be easy if Herod did not fear the loss of the people's favor. In the end, he felt it prudent to keep the Baptist alive though far from Jerusalem to minimize the trouble. King Herod set him free from the dungeons of Jerusalem with the provision that he never re-enter the city, under punishment of death.

John agreed to the king's terms. Water baptism at the River Jordan remained constant in his mind. The day and hour of the Messiah's arrival was near. John wanted to prepare the people.

***

John Baptizes Jeshua

Three days later, hundreds gathered on a very hot morning at the River Jordan. John's devotees waited for their turn to immerse their bodies for the promise of a better life. The passionate words of the Baptist guided the faithful.

Many clapped their hands to the rhythm of drums and the whine of bowed strings, and women shrilled their tongues behind their veils. John held a young girl by the nape of her neck with one hand and her nose by the other. In one single movement, he plunged her beneath the water. She rose and he proclaimed, "Today, young one, I baptize you with water, but one will come after me to baptize you with fire. Now go with the one true God."

She waded to join those who had already experienced the ritual. John greeted the next devotee and stopped. He could no longer hear the music. John stood in the water facing a man who he met with instant recognition. The man's eyes and face were so bright that John could not see his features. His body shook and he could not speak at first. The words came out slowly. "Who are you? Why are you here?"

"I have come to fulfill the law," said Jeshua. "You must baptize me."

"Baptize you? You should be baptizing me, Master."

John knelt in the water and Jeshua placed a hand on his shoulder. "Rise, Baptist, your deliverance is at hand. Help me fulfill the law. You need to baptize me."

John took hold of Jeshua by the neck with a trembling hand. He closed over Jeshua's nostrils and plunged him into the water. On his rising, John spoke. "I baptize you, Lord, with water. Now rise, for our redemption is in your hands."

The music and singing resumed, the silence ending as abruptly as it had begun.

"You have served our Father in Heaven well, John," said Jeshua. "Soon your tribulations will be over."

He waded through the water to the riverbank. John watched him and tears came to his eyes. He raised his hands above his head. "Rejoice my brothers and sisters, for the hour of the Lord has come! On this day God has shown his mercy. Our deliverer, our Messiah is among us!"

***

At the heart of the intrigue, there is always the desire for some action that is self-serving. Caiaphas, alarmed by the actions of the prophet Jeshua, could not expose his concern. This would offer more importance to the man than he thought appropriate.

Instead, he wanted to use the Baptist.

On the morning of the next day, Caiaphas learned of the baptism of Jeshua. He could not contain his satisfaction. A grin spread across his face like a rash, though it appeared to be more like a grimace. The missing piece he had prayed for was given to him.

The collusion between the Baptist and the rabbi would make his plan complete. He had the evidence to charge John the Baptist with acts of sedition and blasphemy. This established that his sanction of the rabbi with the sacred rites upheld by the Counsel was evil under the law.

Caiaphas knew that the Sanhedrin had no authority to put the Baptist to death for his crimes. The Roman procurator would have to listen to the pleas for justice by the Counsel and carry out the sentence. They both owed allegiance to the same ruler, Rome. This public crusade would demonize Jeshua and dissuade him from his self-proclaimed mission. Caiaphas concluded that his actions were perfect and ordained by God.

***

One of the thankless tasks of Procurator is to review the taxes collected from the provinces. Pontius Pilate was going over the accounting when a clatter of voices loomed outside his chambers.

"Centurion, see what the noise is about. I'm trying to concentrate."

The centurion saluted Pilate and left. Soon he returned with a member of the Sanhedrin in tow. "Governor, this priest has an urgent message for your consideration."

Pilate stood and stretched with a sigh. "Very well. I have grown bored with this tedious work anyway."

The priest stepped forward with apologies. "Honorable Procurator, I represent the Counsel of the Sanhedrin with a matter of great importance and utmost urgency. Someone has broken our sacred laws and his crime is punishable by death. Since this is no longer allowed at our discretion, it is a task that your office must carry out on our behalf."

Pilate idly played with the dagger on his desk. "What is the exact nature of this supreme crime?"

"It does not serve the procurator to spend his precious time learning of our laws when it is not his inclination. Allow us our own understandings of the law."

Pilate was annoyed by the priest's condescending attitude. "Indulge me."

"We have certain rites that are sacred to our religion. They are restricted to the priesthood and only those that are ordained may perform these rites. In this case, we have a self-proclaimed prophet performing a sacred rite upon another, who happens to be a rabbi that also proclaims to be the Messiah. He has defiled all of us in the eyes of our God and must be punished. The punishment is death."

Pilate dropped the dagger to the desk. "Let me guess. The man you want punished is the one called John the Baptist?"

The priest nodded in the affirmative.

"And who is the other accomplice in this matter?"

The priest was nervous and reluctant to speak.

Pilate grew impatient. "Priest, I'm waiting."

"The other is the rabbi known as Jeshua, but you need not deal with him. Caiaphas will seek other measures for his indiscretions."

Once again, Jeshua demonstrated his ability to disrupt the peace. Pilate knew that he would have to inform King Herod of this affair before he could proceed. He told the priest he would handle the matter as quickly as possible.

The centurion escorted out the priest while Pilate lingered in thought. He smelled something gone awry, and no doubt a maneuver for political advantage and personal gain. Pilate held no reservations about executing someone who broke the law, whether Roman or Jewish law. Yet despite this, he was obliged to pursue the issue, regardless of his personal opinion.

Pilate sent word to King Herod that he wanted an

audience. Herod returned the messenger with a positive reply. Pilate entered the main hall and called out to the king, but there was no answer. His voice echoed through the palace until a servant approached, bowing to Pilate while he explained, "Governor, we humbly ask your pardon but the king is indisposed at the moment and said that you should wait for him in the antechamber adjacent to his throne.

Pilate motioned for the servant to show him the way. The servant scurried like a rat and he increased his pace to keep up. "Where are the servants this evening?"

"The king was gracious enough to give most of us the night free. I am one of ten in the palace, and others are below tending to their tasks. Please sit and I shall bring you some of the palace wine. Are you hungry?"

Pilate waved off the offer of food and accepted the graciousness of the king's wine. He had no sooner found a place to sit when the king entered. He started to get up and Herod told him to remain seated. "We are friends here. No need for royal protocol at this hour. My friend, what brings you to the palace?"

Pontius accepted the cup of wine from the servant, who waited to hear of the king's desires. King Herod commented, "Assan is one of my finest. There is nothing he will not do for me."

He turned to the servant. "Bring grapes and roast

John Baptizes Jeshua

lamb that we may share. Now Pilate, there must be more than wine my house can serve you. If not food, perhaps the tender caress of a woman. I have many beautiful concubines that would make your skin sing."

Pilate lamented that the offer was faint against some unpleasant business.

"What is so terribly urgent that I cannot dissuade you to other more pleasant considerations?" asked Herod.

Pilate told him of the priest and the business involving the Baptist. Food and more drink arrived and Herod did not hesitate to devour the meat like a ravenous dog, leaving juices and wine to mix into his beard without the least concern for delicacy. He was aloof to the matter as he continued with the food smacking from his jowls and juices dripping from his lips.

"This is what you have brought to me? I was concerned that my borders had been breached by some unspeakable horde, and you bring to me something of little consequence."

Herodias entered the antechamber, hand covering her mouth from a partial yawn. "Did I hear that bastard's name?"

"Now, now... my dear," said Herod. "You must not upset yourself. Pilate was just telling me the Baptist has given trouble to the Jews with his comings and goings."

Herodias was anxious to know if John had violated the king's orders. "Is the bastard in the city? If so, Pilate, you must have him killed at once."

Pilate regarded Herodias. "If you were not the beautiful wife of the king, I should think you have the ferociousness of a Roman soldier and I would make you one of my generals."

The king interrupted. "My friend, I forget you have the prowess to beguile even the savagery of a scorned woman. Let us speak of the demon that plagues the house of Herod and the temple of the Sanhedrin. This is most fortunate, because now I can dispense with him without fear that his fate shall fall solely on me."

"We have to find him. Shall I bring him back to Jerusalem for trial?"

"Oh no," said Herod. "We must not bring him here. Put him into the dungeons of Hebron to rot."

Herodias chimed in. "My dearest king, you shall not rob me of my triumph. I want confirmation of his final humiliation. Let his tongue be removed from his body and his severed head served on a platter with fruit, an apple wedged between his foul jaws like the pig that he is. Do this for me or I shall become as the desert to you, barren and bitter beyond your worst nightmares."

Herod drank her words like poison. "Very well. So

it is said, so it is done. Pilate, follow her instructions."

The next day Pilate ordered the arrest of John the Baptist. By Herod's decree, Pilate sent John to the fortress at Machaerus. Seven months had passed since his release and baptism of Jeshua. On the night he was to be killed, Herod ordered Pilate to give John a Roman death. This meant that John would lose his head. This was Herod's way of honoring John on his own behalf and appeasing what the king believed was John's troubled spirit. This also put an end to Herodias' constant nagging.

The hour before his execution, Jeshua appeared inside his cell and blessed John. He told him that his death was imminent and he promised that he would be with him in his Father's Kingdom in Heaven.

Saul's Gambit

Pontius Pilate considered the growing problem in Judea regarding the proliferation of prophets and seers all claiming to be the one, the messiah foretold in the Hebrew Scriptures. Most were vagrants trying to take advantage of the political situation. He could manage them with the troops available in Jerusalem. There was one that continued to trouble him, especially considering the reports from the centurions returning from Bethany. Prophets performing small feats of magic are one thing, but how this rabbi warded off the centurions was more serious.

Octavius was a seasoned warrior and not easily frightened. Pilate sensed his fear. He trusted Octavius' judgment and estimation of an enemy's strengths and weaknesses. If he described the situation accurately, and there was no reason to think he had not, then the situation was grave indeed. It seemed prudent to warn Rome of the situation even though Pilate wanted to play down the danger.

Before he moved against the rabbi, he wanted confirmation that his judgment had the political backing required to face any ramifications arising from the Sanhedrin's investment in the man. Unrest had caused the ruin of many who had ruled before him. All possible damage that might arise from his decision needed thorough consideration. Tiberius respected Pontius Pilate's caution. He sent a man he thought might be of assistance to Pilate. Tiberius sent Saul of Tarsus.

Saul was an educated man, able to read and write in Latin, Greek, and Aramaic. He had political negotiation experience from time spent on behalf of Rome in Thrace, dealing successfully with the slavery uprisings. He made the political and spiritual complexities of Judea a special focus and knew very well the Hebrew Scriptures. Rome was confident that Saul would provide an independent perspective, while keeping strong liaisons to Rome's interests.

Pilate welcomed Saul's insights into the complexities of Judea's spiritual and social problems, especially since Saul's allegiance was solely to Rome. This dedication he understood and embraced.

Saul arrived in Judea and soldiers escorted him safely to Jerusalem. Once he settled in his quarters, he went to see Pilate. Saul hailed him with his fingers close to his lips as a friendly gesture to offer blessings. "Procurator, I bring greetings from Tiberius on your successful management in this forsaken place of thieves and vipers."

Pontius bowed slightly to honor the emissary from Rome. "Welcome to my humble dwelling, Saul of Tarsus."

"Tell me of this rabbi Jeshua."

"He is an unusual man and possesses unknown power sufficient to ward off the use of force from my centurions. He is a quiet man, moving among the shadows, here in one moment and then a hundred leagues somewhere else, apparently overnight."

Saul sat down and sampled the grapes in a dish on the table near him. He drank the wine presented by Pilate before he spoke again. "Interesting. Does he work alone?"

"At first, I thought as much, but there are rumors that many have taken up with him. I have reports that more than seventy follow him, and crowds pursue him for his magical powers to heal."

"I do not recommend that you confront him yet. It is important to gather evidence of his crimes."

"As I said, his movements are difficult to track because he seems to move at night. Those that follow him will slow him down and make it easier to seize him."

"That will not help. I must get close to him, travel with him, so I can observe his actions at close hand. If he is committing sedition, we need a witness to testify to his crimes."

Pilate was bewildered by this indirect military approach. "How will you get close when only his closest devotees are with him? As a specter of Rome, your reputation is widely known. He will reject you at first sight. You will not get near him. Perhaps someone else is best."

"I must be the one, I alone. Only I can make the necessary accurate reports. I tell you, one such as him can slip through your fingers. This is not about magic. He is just a man who is quite clever."

"So you don't take to the rumors of his magical abilities?"

"He is just a man, only a man. Granted, he is a clever and dangerous, but he is only a man. Any that follow this man Jeshua are nothing more than demented terrorists. I will put them all in jail, and execute as many as I can find."

Pilate realized that Saul had been pursuing Jeshua and his followers long before he was a threat in Judea. Jeshua had become Saul's obsession, and he did not confide in Pilate the rest of his plan.

***

Three days later, Pilate was working to complete the tax collection records when a centurion reported that a man found half dead on the road to Damascas answered to the description of Saul. The centurion said that he was mad from the sun and babbling that he had seen the one true God. His life was changed. When the centurions tried to bring him back to Jerusalem, he refused. He said he had found the Messiah and this was his only mission.

On hearing this, Pilate knew Saul's real plan was about to unfold. The wolf was about to lay down with the lamb. The prophet had met his match. Saul's transformation from the heat of the sun to Paul, the believer, was clever indeed.

Paul and the Disciples

Many months later, Saul, who now wants to be called Paul, came to my quarters in the palace. He informed me of his success to meet the rabbi Jeshua, and he seemed genuinely pleased. I thought for a moment that his enthusiasm was authentic and he had become a believer.

As the evening wore on, Paul revealed how he infiltrated the group. Jeshua was in Capernaum teaching his disciples when a wagon arrived late in the evening, drawn by sympathizers to his cause. Paul lay on a bed of straw in the back of the wagon, weakened from sunstroke.

Those closest to Jeshua heard about Paul's story through a chain of believers from nearby districts and decided to go see for themselves. Saul's transformation and subsequent claim to be Paul appeared as delirium and those that believed in the rabbi fear Paul. They knew about his persecution of the rabbi's followers. They avoided him whenever possible. Eventually they were convinced he spoke from his heart and felt pity for him. They wanted the rabbi to meet with him. Perhaps he could be of help.

Jeshua knew Paul's real motives were not pure but through his spiritual insight could see the significant role he might play in the events to come.

Despite the many conversations Paul and I had, the exact nature of the prophet man Jeshua and his relationship to the mysterious force that overshadows him remain a great mystery to me.

As procurator, I prided myself on my ability to understand the most complex of political intrigues, but this man was beyond my comprehension. I doubted that Paul would ever succeed with his plans simply because Jeshua is no ordinary man. Something works through him that appears supernatural. Despite Paul's cleverness and intelligence, and tenacity, he cannot wrap his mind around this.

The rest of the night Paul unraveled the workings of the inner circle of devotees that Jeshua has collected around him. I was less interested in the prophet man and more in the men he gathered. With the events that took place in Bethany in the back of my mind, I wondered about those men. What were they? I asked myself. Were they also wizards, possessing the power to smite their enemies with a wave of the hand as he had done?

I must keep a watchful eye on these men close to the prophet man. Rumors are spreading that he is the new King of the Jews. My concern was that this new king was gathering an army of wizards to bring down the throne of Judea, and Rome would be next.

Oddly, my prediction about Paul's difficulty in fooling the rabbi was not with the rabbi himself. The difficulty was with his followers. Paul ignored the idea that the rabbi suspected his intentions. He could not see the cleverness of the rabbi in allowing his closest followers to attack him while he sat back and watched. As I listened to Paul's account of his interactions with the members of the inner circle, I experienced a slow and quiet admiration of the prophet man and his diplomatic skill in handling of the situation. My desire to meet him was growing.

Until that opportunity arose, I had to be satisfied with Paul's second-hand references and reflections.

***

On Paul's arrival in the camp of Capernaum, several women cared for him under Jeshua's direction. Even though his condition was partly self-imposed, Jeshua looked in on Paul daily and treated his fevers until they passed. Many of the closest disciples of Jeshua were in the room adjacent to where Paul was resting. He could not help but overhear the complaints lodged against him.

Phillip spoke openly against the persecutor.

"Master, why do you allow this man among us? He has demonstrated many times his true nature and hatred of our beliefs. If it were me, I would have left him to rot in the sun's anvil and say good riddance to him that seeks to slay us in our sleep."

"Can you not see?" asked Jeshua. "In this man are the very issues that you struggle with, issues of betrayal and dishonesty. Search your heart and you will find this to be true. Paul is a mirror and when you gaze into his heart, you become angry that you see yourself. Better we have him among us so he can teach us the meaning of compassion. What good is compassion for your brother if he wrongs you not? The more profound a teaching is to have compassion for the one who wants to harm you, and in his doing so has the possibility to be healed."

Phillip dropped his head at the truth of Jeshua's words. James the Just interjected, "Master, do you intend he stay with us, and if so, will you teach him what you have taught us? Is this knowledge not sacred, Master? Have you not told us that we should be mindful that we should not cast these pearls you have given us before unbelievers that would rebuke us and work to close our hearts?"

Jeshua reflected on James' words. "Brother, we know your heart and the righteousness that flows from it. Yet, fear not. What I have given you is sacred. I want you to revere the teaching I have given you. Know that the teaching does not live beyond you, but inside of you. If I were to bestow the most valuable thing upon the defiler of the truth, he would not have the capacity to understand and make use of it, so it would not matter. The truth can only work through the heart that is open."

Mary the Magdalene spoke. "Brothers, is not the truth for all to hear? You would have the truth held in the hands of the elders without the smallest consideration for the women in the village. Do they not wash your clothes, mend your garments, and cook your meals without seeking your favor? Do they also not have the right to know the truth? Is it right then that we should choose what the Lord God has to say to everyone? Let us be wise and carefully guide Paul to the inner way. I, too, find it difficult to accept his transformation. Yet, I find it difficult to accept my own as well. Is not this about trust?"

She turned to Jeshua with a confident smile.

John interrupted her. "You are a woman. What do you know of these things? Master, I cannot abide by her speaking on your behalf. These are matters for men to deal with."

"You trust a woman to hold you safely in her womb, then why do you not trust that a woman can behold the truth in her bosom?" said Mary. "We must trust ourselves, and each other. No harm shall come to us if we follow the inner way. Are we not strong enough to resist the temptation of the darkness? If Paul is a serpent among us, can he bring down the glory that we feel? If that is so, we should go home now. For we are lost and the Master wastes his time with men and women that are as children frightened so easily in the night."

John would not be moved by her words. "What purpose does a woman serve in the spiritual matters of men? Women should be tending to the hearth and the keeping of the house."

"This woman has clothed you, fed you, and kept you warm by her own means on this long journey. John, you are a child dependant on a woman for your wants and needs. Do you think that the people from other lands know you, love you so much that they would do as much for you as I have done? You would be nibbling on rocks instead of suckling the breasts of my generosity. You would freeze by the desert night, too cold and too weak to bring the word of the Master to anyone. Let your fantasies of spiritual righteousness keep you and see how long you last."

Timothy joined in the debate. "I am not troubled by Paul's presence. I am troubled by the pettiness that seems to disturb the harmony that the Master has tried to achieve within us. We argue and bicker most of the time. Where is the love that he has given us? How can we offer the love we have learned if we cannot love each other? Perhaps we are not ready for the kingdom the Master has described, and undeserving of the love that the Lord God offers."

"Blessed are you, Timothy," said Jeshua. "I tell you all, in this man flows the strength to meet the truth and reach out to the world. He is the rock that gives foundation to my words."

Simon Peter looked hurt. "Lord, I thought I was the one chosen to lead when you are finished here."

"Yes, Peter, it is true. Though I have entrusted you with our brothers' future welfare after I am gone, you will deny me three times before the cockcrows.

"Impossible, Master. I would never deny you," he said emphatically.

Jeshua turned to Mary and lovingly caressed her hand as he spoke. "Brothers, my love for you knows no bounds but before you stands a vessel that holds the light of the world. In her, I have given the cup of my blood, the hope of life everlasting, the seed of my seed, heart of my heart. In her, I entrust all that I am forever more.

"I tell you a great truth. The Alpha and Omega must begin within the divine feminine. All that manifests begins within the womb of transgression."

Paul emerged and leaned on a tree limb, partially

covered by bed wrappings. "Brothers, I have heard your harsh words. I cannot blame you for not trusting me. I have a terrible history. But I have been reborn. God has shown me the error of my ways and I have repented my sins. I only want to be a part of this great endeavor. I want to learn from the Master about the inner way of the open heart. Let me do my humble part.

"I have much to offer. My ability to read and write important languages and my connections to Rome can only be of help to you. Rome does not understand the truth behind this movement. Who is better equipped than I to communicate your mission to those who do not understand your way?"

Jeshua waited to see if there were any more comments.

Bartholomew threw up his hands. "So that is it? We are going to let this monster into our family? I do not agree. You don't just spend years hunting down and executing our people and then one day decide you were wrong and turn around to say you are a believer. Paul is a goat and will always be a goat. Call me what you want, but I cannot abide this. I'm sorry, Master."

He stormed out of the group and Mark called after him.

"Let him go," said Jeshua. "He'll come around eventually. Whatever your personal feelings are about this, we must yield to the wisdom of the Father who is in heaven. He knows best for all concerned. We must yield to His will if we are to proceed."

The disciples nodded with some reluctance to Jeshua's advice.

Jeshua Weds Mary

In the rooms of Pontius Pilate in Jerusalem, Paul told of the marriage he had witnessed. He had joined the inner circle of disciples and Jeshua, and then traveled to Antioch. A marriage ceremony was planned in the village for the following evening.

Paul thought that the family had prearranged the marriage with Jeshua before they arrived. Later he learned the ceremony was between Jeshua and Mary the Magdalene. He was astonished by this unusual behavior.

That the prophet man dared to have a relationship with a prime disciple was significant, but more shocking to learn was that he taught the scriptures and had spiritual dialogues with a woman. In Judea, women were never allowed to enter the synagogue, read, or even discuss the Torah. Paul explained to Pilate that it was also forbidden for rabbis to imbibe wine or marry. Normally, he said, they devoted themselves to a life of service within the religion.

Once again, the prophet man never ceased to amaze Pilate. He smiled at all of what Paul told him. Paul was disturbed by the prophet man's relationship to the woman. First, that he would marry her, and second, that she was with child before they were betrothed. This was unthinkable and blasphemous to Paul.

Paul made no effort to hide his negative feelings about the woman Mary. He stated on more than one occasion that she was a harlot, an abomination, and deserved to be stoned according to Mosaic Law. He dared not to mention this to the prophet man lest he anger him and threaten Paul's plans. Paul was not the only one who felt this way, even after Jeshua chastised his flock by saying, "Let him who is without sin cast the first stone."

At one point, Paul described the prophet man as an evil priest. He expressed judgment that he should be cast out of the clergy for his shameful and evil ways. His behavior at the wedding was disgraceful.

"Paul, is this not what you expected of this man?" Pilate asked. "It seems that you have more than enough to bring this man to justice."

"Yes, from a purely scriptural point of view but we need to prove sedition and that is more troublesome."

"I have heard him called the King of the Jews. Is this true?"

"Yes." Paul said. "However, this does not come from his lips. He is clever in the way he turns around a statement. He says to the people, 'You have said these things, but these are not my words.' "

"There is but one king in this part of Judea, Herod. If he is proclaiming his right to rule over Herod, then he seeks to undermine Herod's rule and this is sedition."

"The zealots are the key. If we could somehow catch him in the act of supporting their cause against Rome then we have grounds for capture and punishment."

Paul paused as if lost in thought. His eyes turned distant and hollow.

"Is there something troubling you?" asked Pilate.

"He actually got up to dance, in front of everyone. It was shameful, simply shameful. And then..." Paul's face changed color.

"What is it my friend? Tell me."

"The celebration had gone on for hours, and more than a hundred people were present, with at least three barrels of wine already consumed. One disciple approached Jeshua to inform him that there was no more wine. I believe it was Matthew, or Andrew. No matter. It was strange what happened in that moment..." Again, Paul's eyes went vacant.

"What is it, man? By the gods tell me."

"Jeshua pointed to the barrels leaning against the wall. Matthew explained to Jeshua that he already checked them and they only contained water. Jeshua told him to check again. Matthew was frustrated and hurt by his remark. He shrugged his shoulders and begrudgingly returned to the barrels. He uncovered each lid to find they now had wine. Six barrels and everyone full of wine. How do you suppose he did that?"

Pilate could see Paul's troubled face. He did not know what to say to his story. He remembered the story that Octavius told of this rabbi's power in Bethany to smite a centurion with a wave of his hand.

"Is this man a god in human form?" Pilate declared in anger.

Paul did not answer.

Pilate was disturbed by this casual and vulgar display of power and began to wonder. A shudder of fear entered his heart. "Who is this man? What kind of man could do this?' he asked himself.

Paul added to Pilate's bewilderment regarding Jeshua and his ability to perform unbelievable feats of magic.

Several weeks after Jeshua and the disciples left Antioch, they arrived at Jamneith, not far from Gaulanitis. Many had gathered knowing that the rabbi was going to speak to the people. Some had traveled from as far as the Arnon River and Etam. They did not think of the journey and the toll upon themselves. They were hungry for his words, and for food.

Andrew and Escham told the rabbi that they had

little to feed these people. The rabbi asked for the baskets of their food from their journey from Antioch.

Andrew said, "Master, we have but a few loaves of bread and a handful of fish left. We cannot feed these people. We should send them away."

"Be not afraid," said Jeshua. "Our Father's table is always bountiful to those who seek his love and light. If you ask for a loaf of bread, or a piece of cheese, do you think that he shall offer a stone?"

Paul bowed his head. He recomposed his feelings and said, "The rabbi muttered a prayer of sorts as he waived his hand over the baskets. He concluded with, 'and Your will be done.'

"It was amazing. We saw it happen. He told Escham to dump the baskets out on the ground and give the food to the people. Bread, cheese, and fish poured out as though the baskets had no bottom. After many hours, all of the people had their fill and more."

Pilate stared at Paul. He wanted to dispel the moment and declined to accept what Paul was saying. Like it or not, he could not erase the expression on Paul's face.

"My friend, it is late. You have a long journey ahead of you in the morning. Let us take our leave and rest. We will talk of this again soon. I have much to think about."

Paul bid Pilate a good night.

Jeshua's Temptation

*P*aul's plan to entrap the rabbi was his own private business. I wanted to know of the rabbi's plans and movements, his strategies for conquest and his plan to overthrow Rome. These were my primary concerns. Paul had a strange obsession, another agenda going well beyond the rabbi. Only time would tell exactly how that would play out.

***

To Pilate's surprise, Paul was gone by morning. He expected to talk more of the rabbi before he departed, perhaps over something to eat. Paul left without saying a word. Later that morning, a manservant delivered a note he found in Paul's quarters:

"Sorry to leave you friend, but I felt it urgent to return without further delay. I will contact you at the earliest opportunity. Paul."

Paul returned to the disciples' camp at Philoteria near the Sea of Galilee and found the disciples waiting for the rabbi's arrival. Jeshua had awakened in the night and departed for the desert before daybreak. Only James the Lesser knew of the Master's plan to enter into the desert alone. Paul wanted to follow but James was insistent.

"The Master wanted to be alone on his journey to meditate and contemplate his ministry in Jerusalem," said James.

Paul asked how long Jeshua had been gone. James told him the Master had been away for three days. He also said that there was no way to know how long he planned to be in the desert.

The disciples grew impatient. Jeshua did not return as expected. Thomas, known for his negative perspective, suggested that the desert might have overwhelmed him. Perhaps he lay dead. The idea was quickly rejected and Thomas posed a question, "How would we know what to do or where to go if he is lost?"

They argued among themselves and Simon Peter commiserated as well. These were practical and simple men. It was difficult for them to admit their real concerns. They felt lost. They worried about the Master and why he had abandoned them near the shores of Galilee.

Peter gathered them as if they were fish in his nets. The disciples began to stray and talk of leaving, and he firmly reminded them that the Master said to wait for his return. Peter's words were comforting. He brought a steadiness to the group. They listened to Peter because he made sense. His ability to stand fast and hold was his true strength. His patience was derived from being a good fisherman.

Paul sat alone on the shore and composed letters to Pilate, relaying the situation and updating him on their movements, plans, and general mood.

***

On the fortieth day, there was still no sign of Jeshua. The disciples were angry. They thought of family members left behind, their flocks and fields abandoned. Some wondered how the Master could abandon them and leave behind the pregnant Mary he cared about.

For three years they had followed the Master from one village to the next. The disciples grumbled a little but to their credit did not look back. They thought of their more important mission of bringing the Father's will upon the earth. They watched as He called people from their homes and as He spoke to those who would listen.

He quoted scripture from the Torah and spoke in riddles. The disciples wondered about this strange behavior. While many tried to understand the Master's intentions, Mark and John asked Jeshua why he did not freely give his wisdom to the people.

Jeshua replied, "The masses are as sheep and sleep through their lives. They live in fear and focus their attention on tradition and the old laws of Moses. They do not think for themselves and would not embrace the truth if given to them as I speak to you. Therefore, I give them stories and riddles so that they may define themselves as ready. It is the way of the ancient and wise."

There were many discussions about Roman rule. The subject often came up from the people. They questioned that if Jeshua is the One, the true Messiah, then when was the hour of their deliverance? Rome's oppression was apparent to the disciples as they traveled across Judea.

They moved about to avoid the violence around them. Mary arranged for their passage and their lodgings, made possible by her influence and financial means. Meanwhile, Jeshua taught them to love one another, to be kind and compassionate, even to their enemies.

Many struggled to understand this as it applied to the cruel Roman behavior prevalent in their lives. The disciples spoke openly about using their new knowledge to work against Roman rule. Jeshua quickly declined that approach. Taxation was also a sore point among many. Jeshua befriended the tax collectors and spent many hours discussing spiritual truths with them. No one liked the tax collectors. They were perceived as collaborators, guilty of robbing the poor for the oppressors. James was often critical of Jeshua about this problem. Jeshua commented, "Brothers, you cannot change these things and must render to Caesar what is Caesar's. To uphold the law is to honor the Father."

"How can you abide by these vermin that practice rape of what little the people possess?" James responded. "You treat them kindly as if they are like us. Is this righteousness?"

"Are these also not men of equal value? They suffer in the darkness as you and know not the truth. Can you hold them ransom that they must pay for their sins in their unconsciousness? Where is the justice? I tell you, by the Father in heaven, he knows them not and there is no meaning to him about this."

Jeshua spoke often of the Heavenly Father, and the role of the disciples in spreading His word. He offered many insights into the world of spirit and the nature of life beyond death. These discussions led to many arguments and preoccupied their minds during Jeshua's absence. Now they had run out of disagreements. Worries over their direction and purpose should Jeshua never return, grew more each day until they became intolerable.

The group split into factions and warred with words against each other about whether to go or stay. The frustration mounted beyond Peter's ability to moderate. Just when all seemed to fall apart, Jeshua appeared at the summit of a nearby sand dune. Peter sat down, saddened and ashamed of his lack of control, as Timothy raised his hand and staff to yell "The Master returns! Blessed be, blessed be. Hah-Leh, Hah-Leh, Yod Ha!"

Many fell to their knees and wept. Disagreements were forgotten and all was well again. Mary ran to him, holding her belly laden with his child. As she reached Him, she fell and grasped at his knees. He lifted her up and they embraced. Her actions were for everyone. There were no adequate words to express their rejoicing.

Paul wrote to Pilate another letter about Jeshua's experience of strange spiritual encounters in the desert. At night, while deep in meditation, spirits appeared. He described them as Djinn, the ancient ones. They knew of his intentions to bring transformation and redemption. They spoke of the evildoers, the oppressors of his people. They said, "Jeshua, you are the chosen among men. Revel in your time. You are to lead your people to a new kingdom. It is your kingdom. You are the king, the king of these people. Men are ignorant of the truth that you speak and must be shown the way. It must be the way of the ax and spear. Your love is commendable, but it is not enough. The darkness is great among the oppressors and they only know of strength. Use what you have been given to free them, to rule with your wisdom."

After his return, Jeshua talked of going among the people to remind them of the treachery of the Romans and their cruelty, to rally them to rise up against the Romans in a united front. He spoke of rebellion, of the righteousness of the zealots. The role of the disciples was to lead the people against the Romans until all were free. Some were enthusiastic and others were confused. Thomas, one of the youngest, expressed his doubt.

"Master, I do not understand. You spoke of love and compassion toward our enemies. Now you speak about striking out against them. How do you reconcile the difference?"

"Thomas, you are the least of those here," answered Jeshua. "I admire your candor and willingness to stand for your beliefs, and mostly your honesty. You are pure of heart and truly you will come to know the Father. It is true that I taught you about love.

"I believe that it is the key element needed in the lives of men to bring them to the truth. Yet at the same time, the Romans are a brutal and formidable force. The Pharisees and Sadducees are pompous, full of pride. They align with the Roman influence for their own purposes. They fail to understand the love I bring and my teaching will not persuade them to change."

"Master, though I am young and inexperienced, I believe in what you are saying. I am passionate about what you are doing. Nevertheless, I am weak. I fear I cannot stand against these dark forces. I will fail you, Lord."

Jeshua turned to Simon Peter. "Procure me a boat that will hold as many of us that stand here."

"As you wish. I have many friends that fish in Galilee. They will give me a boat if I ask."

Jeshua said, "Then make it so and quickly."

Peter returned hours later, just as the sun slumped past the horizon. He beckoned Jeshua and all of the disciples to follow him. Along the shore sat a large boat, 15 leagues in length, and loaded with several sets of oars. It was fitted with a single mast with sails lashed around the middle, with many fishing nets piled on the bottom toward the bow.

Jeshua told the disciples to get in the boat and raise the sails, while he directed the others that stayed behind to push the boat out to sea. Soon the evening tide carried out the boat. Dark clouds formed overhead, indicating that a big storm approached.

Those disciples who were not fishermen were troubled by the storm. They wondered if Jeshua was planning their demise on the sea. Peter happily unfurled the sails and greeted the winds that blew through his robes and hair as old friends. The rest huddled together. They clutched the sides of the boat with fear as the waves thrashed and pitched the boat, splashing water over those inside.

Jeshua climbed over the nets and took a position with his feet planted on the bow. He raised his hands above him and yelled, "Beshud, Ah-che-leh-heh, Man-O-him, spirit of the airs and waters, I command you to be still!"

The wind calmed and the sea became quiet. A strange and dark quiet surrounded them. Jeshua climbed out of the boat and waded through the water ten leagues from the boat. He stood without plunging into the waters below his feet. The disciples stared wide-eyed.

Jeshua called to Thomas. "Climb out of the boat and come to me."

"Oh, Master," said Thomas. "I am terribly afraid."

"Do you trust me? If so, then come to me now."

"But Master, I have already told you my faith is weak."

"Thomas, I am waiting. Will you keep your Master waiting?"

Thomas climbed out of the boat assisted by his brothers and waded through the water with his eyes fixed on Jeshua. He reached half way and looked down on the water, and became frightened. Thomas fell into the water. He surfaced long enough to scream out that he could not swim.

Jeshua swept Thomas from the water and carried him to the boat. The brothers hauled him in and laughed at what a big catch they had made. Peter said, "You would make a fine fish. You even smell of fish."

The disciples laughed and broke the silence that hovered over them. Jeshua proclaimed to all, "Now my brothers, as you can see, even if your faith is the size of a small seed, you can reduce the largest mountain to rubble, and rule the elements. Simon Peter, shift the boom so that we may make way for the shore."

Peter nodded to Jeshua's request. That evening they all slept soundly on the shores of Galilee.

The letters from Paul reporting the incident astounded Pilate. He could hardly believe the words. Yet, Pilate knew Paul was not prone to exaggeration. Pilate was troubled about the power demonstrated by the prophet man. His desire to meet this mystery man grew by every day that passed. Paul also told him that the rabbi planned to enter Jerusalem soon. Pilate anticipated the chance to question the rabbi face to face.

First Meeting

Flavius Senacus came to my quarters early in the morning. It had been a late night for me, flavored by a significant abuse of house wine and the affections of a concubine. My head had yet to cease spinning, let alone give a clear view of the day.

Senacus, hardened by years of guarding the frontier, welcomed any opportunity to return to Rome. When a new assignment to lead part of the garrison at Jerusalem presented itself, he saw the chance for a triumphant return to Rome with Judea neatly tucked under his helmet. His arrogance and impudence exceeded his zeal, as he never knew loss or failure. Therefore, I could not fault him. Also, to his credit, his men respected and looked up to him.

He is a good choice, a fine officer, but I knew that the desert would eventually have its way with him and temper his arrogance.

The brightness of the morning did not match the exuberance displayed by this soldier, so eager to please. His voice echoed loud, far too loud in my ears.

***

"Must you rob me of any peace this early morning?" demanded Pilate.

"I humbly ask your pardon, but I have urgent news from beyond the city walls," said Senacus.

Pilate tried to be gracious over his physical pain. "Very well, what is it that is so urgent that it should have my undivided attention?"

"You wanted news of the rabbi's movements. He will approach the city gates within the hour."

Pilate whipped his head around, causing him to wince. "Is he armed? How many are with him?"

"He does not seem armed. In fact, he rides a donkey. Hundreds of men, women, and children walk before him, dancing, singing, and waving olive branches and date palm leaves."

Pilate pondered to himself. "Does this man take me for a fool? What a clever strategy, I'll give him that, though not what I expected."

"The men who are with him, are they armed?" Pilate barked.

"They appear to be farmers and fishermen dressed in common clothing. We did not see any weapons. Do you want us to apprehend him? If we capture him now, I'm sure we can manage the rest."

Pilate sighed. "Not yet. Let us not show our hand

too soon. Let him come into the city. We have plenty of soldiers if need be. We can afford to be magnanimous and allow him to make the first move. Have centurions ready to surround the main square just in case."

Senacus smacked his armor. "By your command, Governor."

***

Jeshua sat on his donkey, waving to onlookers as they passed his band of happy followers. He wanted to enter into Jerusalem showing his humble attitude and peaceful intention. At the city walls, many gathered around the procession in awe. They were curious about the rabbi who rode a donkey, a sight they were unaccustomed to.

The centurions kept a watchful eye for any signs that His entrance was a ruse for a zealot attack. Jeshua entered the gates of the city and continued to the Great Temple where he wanted to offer prayers. The zealots planned an assault to match his arrival at the temple. They hoped that He would raise his hand to bring the Romans to their knees and assure victory for the zealots.

Pilate looked down from his palace window as Jeshua and His followers walked toward the Temple near the city square. The singing, dancing, and cheering dazzled the crowds, and some joined in not knowing the reason for the procession. When Pilate saw this, he said to himself, "The prophet man draws the crowd easily. They are mesmerized by this beggar's charm. I find it hard to believe that this is the man Paul wrote to me about. He hardly seems kingly sitting on that ridiculous donkey."

The crowd stopped when Jeshua dismounted the donkey and climbed the steps to the temple's entrance. Simon Peter, Simon the Zealot, and Timothy followed Jeshua as he entered the porch. In front of Jeshua sat moneychangers exchanging Roman money stamped with the seal of Tiberius. The new Roman law, instituted by Pontius Pilate, declared that all coinage used in the realm must be marked by the emperor's image. This made for a problem at the Great Temple. Tithing and donations could not have a graven image. Therefore, on the porch, priests exchanged the graven-imaged coins for shekels.

Jeshua understood the need for this, but what he saw made him angry. He went to a table and inquired, "Tell me priest, I have ten denarius. How many shekels will you give me in exchange?"

The priest cut short his negotiation over another tribute, and answered Jeshua, "I shall give you six half shekels for your ten denarius, rabbi."

"Why do you give me so little for what I have offered?"

The priest shrugged his shoulders. "I am giving you the going price. The exchange is fair."

Jeshua yelled with frustration. "You have turned my Father's house into a den of thieves and robbers. This is not fair. This is an abomination in a holy place."

He grabbed the priest's table and turned it upside down, and proceeded to the next table, overturning it as well. Jeshua ran from table to table and swept the coins on to the stone floor. As he rampaged, the priests bellowed at Jeshua. "What are you doing? You have no right to disrupt our dealings. This is the house of God and you are committing sacrilege."

"I have every right," said Jeshua. "My words are from My Father in Heaven."

"Blasphemer!" said the priests in return.

The crowd became riled and it was no longer safe. Simon suggested to Timothy they get Jeshua away from the temple, as a larger skirmish took place in the middle of the square.

The zealots took Jeshua's rampage in the temple as a sign to execute their attack on the Romans. From underneath their robes, they drew swords and began to slaughter the soldiers. Blood ran over the cobblestones in the streets. Soon more soldiers poured into the square to fight the zealots.

Barabbas, leader of the revolt, watched Jeshua climbing the steps away from the riot. He called out to the rabbi. "Unleash your power and liberate your people. It is time to proclaim that you are King."

Jeshua looked at the violence exploding before him. "I am truly sorry. I was wrong to deceive you. Violence is not the way of the Father. Love is the only way...I can see that now. I'm sorry."

"Why, Master? You said the axe and spear was the answer," asked Simon the Zealot. "I told them you would lend your support."

"I was mistaken, Simon. Forgive me."

Jeshua disappeared beyond the citadel, while more centurions surrounded the square and started to systematically slaughter the rebels. Barrabas escaped the death trap but was later captured, along with two of his co-conspirators. Then the soldiers took them to prison.

Word reached Pontius Pilate that Jeshua did not join the revolt. This confused Pilate and gave him greater curiosity about the prophet man. He sent out word to call Jeshua to the palace for an audience. Two hours passed until Octavius came to Pilate's quarters with the report that the rabbi was waiting to meet him.

Pilate finished his bath. His manservants dressed him in a toga and provided him with wine. He was ready to receive his honored guest.

"Bring him in," he said. Jeshua entered his quarters.

"Please, you are welcome here. Unlike most priests, I understand you are not averse to imbibing a little wine?"

Jeshua nodded in the affirmative.

Pilate beckoned his manservant to bring more wine. "Have a seat. Let us talk of your mission in Judea. I have watched you from afar and I am intrigued by your travels."

Jeshua looked at Pilate. "Why does the procurator of Judea find my ministry of interest? Do you seek after the truth?"

"It is my business to know the truth about all of what goes on in Judea. With that said, may I ask if it is true you have proclaimed yourself King of the Jews?"

Jeshua gazed into Pilate's eyes. Pilate was unnerved by the silence. "Rabbi, are you the new King of the Jews?"

"Is this to be a conversation or an interrogation?" answered Jeshua.

"Understand my position. If there is a new king to be crowned, as procurator I must know these things. I am sure this would be of interest to the monarch already sitting on Judea's throne."

"I have not said this, only my followers. My

kingdom is my Father's and it does not exist here."

Pilate digested the answer. "You caused quite a stir at the temple. I understand your feelings about the Pharisees, and I do not care much for their company. Frankly, I was concerned that your outrage would disturb the Roman peace in Jerusalem. I was happy to see that you were not the leader of seditious zealots, as it had been rumored."

"I am about the business of the Father in heaven," said Jeshua. "I am not concerned by the political issues that concern Rome."

"Now that is good news. I should hate to think we would be enemies before we have come to know each other."

"All men are my brothers. I am here to remind them of their inheritance."

"What do you mean by inheritance? Do you include Roman soldiers? I do not recall having anyone leave me a fortune."

"The Father does not care about your soldiering. It is something that you do just like my father Joseph carpentered. Yet both of you are equal in the eyes of the Father."

"Is your Father so rich that he can afford to give to all mankind?"

"The Father is without limit in his abundance. But it is not worldly riches I am talking about."

"What other riches are there? A man should be able to look forward to a life of luxury as a reward for his efforts."

Jeshua looked at Pilate.

"Do not seek after this world's rewards. This world's riches will be bitter in your belly and give sweetness only in your mouth while they leave you hungry. I tell you this shall pass away from you as surely as your body will return to dust. The wise seek the glory of the Father, and all other things will be provided accordingly."

Pilate remained silent for a moment. "Do you always speak in riddles, prophet?"

"Let him see who has eyes to see and hear who has ears to hear. The truths I speak of have your heart as their target, leaving your mind to waste away in the dust. The truth comes like a thief in the night to take away your comfort and leave you troubled, in order that you may fill your lamp with oil to shatter the darkness that fills your spirit and lay waste to the illusions of your mind."

Pilate turned the cup of wine in his hand. He wanted to understand this strange man. Jeshua seemed friendly enough, but he could not shake what the prophet had done to his soldiers in Bethany.

Jeshua smiled. "I find it is very common to fear what you do not fully understand. You are troubled by what I have done in Bethany...be not afraid. I meant no harm to him who tried to stop me from completing my Father's business."

Disarmed by Jeshua's ability to read his thoughts, Pilate waited to speak. "Is it true that you have the power to restore life out of death?"

"Under certain circumstances it is possible to restore life to one who is vacant for a short time. The cycle of life and death is a matter of course. I simply wanted to show that with the Father there is life everlasting, once life on Earth has ceased to have meaning."

Pilate was unsure as to how to handle the prophet. He wanted to know more about Jeshua and was surprised to notice that a genuine personal interest in the prophet man had developed within him. Before the conversation, Pilate was confident that he could trap him into an admission of guilt and confirm his role as an enemy of Rome. Now he was not so sure. Worse, he liked the man.

He reasoned that he wanted to know his enemy better, to understand his tactics before he pounced on him. Pilate had lost his hold on this mystery man. Jeshua was in his quarters sitting before him, yet Pilate knew that it was Jeshua who had him in his grasp.

This man would not be defeated with the sword,

but with his wits. The only way to bring him down would be to find fault with his teaching. Pilate made up his mind. He would speak with him again and engage him in a deeper discussion about his beliefs in this Father of his. To meet the rabbi on his own ground would become his greatest triumph. Brilliant strategy was necessary to undermine the rabbi's confidence.

Pilate was the better soldier. He regarded his opponent and confirmed that Jeshua was not a soldier. Battle strategy was Pilate's greatest attribute, learned from Gaius Aurelias and Pompeii.

He stood up and set down his cup of wine. "This conversation is over, at least for now. Make yourself available as I may want to speak with you on some other day, rabbi."

Jeshua placed his cup next to Pilate's. "I look forward to meeting you again. My business has just begun here in Jerusalem so I will be easy to find."

He turned and walked toward the door. Before his exit, he made a gesture with his fingers and said, "Peace be with you, brother."

The rabbi took the air with him as he left Pilate. It was hard to breathe. Pilate tried to remember their words. It was like a soldier checking his body for serious wounds after a battle. He could not shake the suspicion that he had lost the first round. How could a simple rabbi outflank a seasoned general?

This prophet man managed to entangle Pilate with some of his magic guile. Jeshua was more dangerous than he originally surmised. The next meeting with the prophet man would be different.

Peter Versus Mary

*P**aul continued to write letters to me about the workings of the inner circle of the rabbi's followers and especially about his wife, Mary. He did not care much for her, as she was outspoken, often abusive to him and the rest, self-righteous to a fault, and believed the rest coveted her close relationship with Jeshua. His letters have many complaints of her actions.*

He wrote that Mary was close to her expected time for birthing their child. With only two months left of her time to carry, she brewed tea with special herbs she gathered from the caravans from the east. The herbs were helpful to pregnant women. They helped ease the pain and kept up a woman's strength in the final days of carrying.

Jeshua had returned from the palace. According to Paul, the first meeting with me encouraged him. He told Mary that though I was not supportive, I was not the hardened man many had led him to believe.

***

Many of the disciples expressed fear that public declaration of Jeshua's ministry was not only foolish but also dangerous. John, James, and Phillip, who were closest to Jeshua, agreed they must move cautiously within the gates of Jerusalem. The word on the street was that they had already developed many enemies. The most prevalent reports were of great distrust from the ranks of the Pharisees inside the Sanhedrin.

Jeshua did not agree. He believed whole-heartedly in his mission, and the power and influence of the Christ force to be unstoppable. Mary had questions. "Have you not said that there is a time for everything and all things flow from the ease? Why do you push so hard, my love? Is it God's will that this must happen so quickly, or is it your pride and self will that empowers this acceleration?"

Jeshua bowed his head. "I will not be counseled by my wife before the Father. Why do you not trust? I tell you it has its own momentum. I merely follow, woman."

"If you move too fast, people cannot digest what is given. They need time to know this new way. They are full of traditions, my love. They do not give them up as easily as you or I," pleaded Mary. "I, too, am afraid. Not for you, but I feel that their fears will rule their hearts more than your love can console."

Jeshua pushed her red hair from her face. "Your eyes are brighter than any of the emeralds I have seen being worn by the sultans of the East, and matched by the fire that burns in your locks. Be not afraid, Mary."

"Jerusalem is different. These people are not the simple people we have met in the many villages. These people are hardened and learned, jaded with a lust for power and wealth. They are full of pride and arrogance, and they do not see the beauty of the spirit that burns inside your heart."

She placed her hand on his breast and he covered her hand with his. Mary continued. "My fear is that they will not understand what you are trying to do." Tears trailed down her cheeks.

Jeshua kissed her forehead and hugged her close when she let out a brief cry.

"What is it? Are you alright?" Jeshua urged.

"I believe he kicked me," she remarked with a giggle.

Jeshua placed his warm hand upon her belly to feel the new life squirming to be free. They smiled at each other in recognition of the miracle they had created together. Their focus on the child's movement washed away the concerns about Jeshua and Jerusalem. Mary fell asleep in his arms.

Jeshua needed to resolve an issue between Simon Peter, now called Peter, and Matthew. He left Mary to sleep, and joined Peter to meet with Matthew at his family home. Peter judged Matthew harshly because of his history as a tax collector for the Romans. He tried to comply with Jeshua's command to love his brother as he would love himself, but could not get past the fact that Matthew had been accepted as a disciple. He believed like so many other Jews, even though Matthew was also a Jew, that he was a sinner against the people of Israel.

Peter and Jeshua arrived at Matthew's home and the women rushed to greet Jeshua. They dipped their hair in water and began to bath his feet from the dust and dirt. Matthew remarked, "You always have your way with the women. I never get my feet washed, not even by my wife when I was home."

Jeshua laughed. "Perhaps you are not willing to give to them what I am willing to give to them."

"And what would that be, Master?"

"You do not give them respect. You expect them to care for you because it is their lot in life. I honor them and admire their beauty in giving."

Matthew grunted in disagreement. Peter sat down next to Jeshua, uncomfortable at being in the tax collector's household. The atmosphere became noticeably chilled. The whole family witnessed Peter's disdain. Jeshua gathered everyone around to tell a story. He learned this from the masters in the East who taught him about the truth.

Jeshua addressed the others in the room and ignored Peter and Matthew.

"There were once two brothers. They both lived and worked in their father's house. While the first brother kept the records and accounting, the second brother carried out the menial chores that maintained the household and lands. In time, the second brother grew very jealous of the first brother. He coveted his brother's task because he worked shorter days and did not become soiled from his work. At the same time, the second brother believed he was pious and better than the first. He performed his duties everyday without fail and never asked anything in return. He saw his duties as more important to the father. At the same time, the father knew that both brothers were essential to the wealth and success of the household. He told them that if they loved and supported one another, they would both benefit from their work, because their work would increase the inheritance their father prepared for them."

Jeshua looked at Peter and then at Matthew. "The Father holds for both of you the promise of his inheritance. He loves you and wants you to flourish. He sees within your heart a desire to love and offer good works and fellowship. Look beyond this place and care not for what you will do or for what you get in return. It has nothing to do with the value of your spirit. I implore you, let go of your hatred. Forgive them whom you believe have trespassed against you, just as you would ask the Father to forgive your trespasses against Him."

Peter wept in shame. He held his head in his hands and pulled on his hair as he lamented. Matthew embraced him and they wept together.

Jeshua left them. Peter returned to the inn where they all stayed, leaving Matthew to enjoy his family. Peter found Mary gathering Thomas' clothing. She said nothing when he entered and he was irritated by the lack of acknowledgment.

"Why do you care for Thomas as though he were your child?"

"He is a grown man," said Mary. "He is not my child."

"Yet you do this for him just the same. Why?"

"I do this out of love. He is a young man who does not yet know to do these things for himself. He has yet to find a woman to take care of him, so I do these things for now."

"If you so love, woman, why not do this for all of us? It is what you are best suited for, is it not?"

"It's a wonder, Peter, that Jeshua set you before us as leader when you are least capable of speaking the right words."

Peter became enraged. "There it is! I have said many times, you strut around with your pride and arrogance, staring down your nose at us because you have the privilege of reading and writing down the words. You waste your money on silly things, unimportant things. I cannot abide that the Master considers you the most blessed among us, and how you hide behind his robes of authority."

Mary resisted raising her voice to a man. Her father had been adamant about respecting men. It was so important in their dealings from the caravans. Still she had to speak her mind. "Peter, you are the most ignorant man I have ever laid eyes on. I cannot abide by the fact that an illiterate ignorant man has the task of organizing and managing Jeshua's closest followers."

Peter snapped, "Listen to me, woman. Though you have beguiled the Master, you do not fool me for a moment. Women have no business in the spiritual affairs of men. As a fisherman, I have the patience and the steadiness to gather these men just fine. I have had many fine catches to my credit and this is no different. As the Master says, I am a fisher of men. I have hand-picked the disciples and they are good men."

Mary's words had struck their mark. "I think the fish jumped into your nets and you had nothing to do with it."

Peter remembered feeling the same way. When he spent many hours at sea, he often felt God rewarded him for being patient in the waiting and preparing for the catch of the day.

Peter finally said, "Woman, you have a mouth like a viper and more stubbornness than a donkey unwilling to carry his load. Perhaps the Master sees in you what I have just witnessed. You have wisdom beyond your years. I give you that. You are merely a jewel that needs polishing."

"Perhaps you are a stone that one day will become a jewel that needs polishing," said Mary.

He shrugged his shoulders. "You are impossible. Women are the reason I preferred to be at sea, where the waves and the salt air soothed a poor man's heart."

Paul wrote to Pilate that banter like this between Mary and the disciples would go on for days, as well as with him. Pilate sympathized with Paul as he read the letter. Paul needed to endure that woman's wrath to accomplish his goal.

Further Dialogues

Late in the afternoon, King Herod summoned Pontius Pilate to the throne room is a state of agitation.

"You do not keep us informed," said Herod. "I want to know the exploits of the rabbi. There are rumors. Must I resort to listening to rumors to know of his performing miracles? What do you know of this?"

"I have one who lives with them. He acts as a spy. His name is Paul. He pretends to be a disciple of the rabbi. Through letters, he provides me with reports of the rabbi's activities," answered Pilate.

"Who is this Paul you speak of?"

"He is also known as Saul of Tarsus."

"Yes, the scribe from Rome. I know him. Is he not a persecutor of these rebels? How could he be one of them?"

Pilate took a breath. "It is complicated, but he has managed to convince them he has changed and is now accepted as one their own."

"I see. Tell me of these feats of magic I keep hearing about. Is it true that he can bring the dead back to life, walk on water, and heal the infirmed?"

Pilate was troubled to answer the king. "I have received letters from Paul that he witnessed the events you speak of. I, for one, have difficulty accepting these reports at face value. As procurator, I must pay attention to any activity within my jurisdiction, yet I am reluctant to accept what I hear about the rabbi as the truth. I prefer to have these stories corroborated by others who are present as well."

"Is it not also true this rabbi has proclaimed himself to be king?"

"I have also heard it said, but when I asked the rabbi directly, he denied any such claim," Pilate consoled. "King Herod, these stories are utterly unbelievable. No one to my knowledge has ever been able to accomplish such feats, even a wizard. I have met this man and it is my impression that he is just a man, another prophet like all the rest and nothing more."

King Herod was disappointed by Pilate's estimation of the prophet man. He got up from his throne and paced for a few moments while he digested Pilate's words.

"Very well...Let us see what this man is about. Bring him to me so I might question him directly. I will make him prove that he has magical powers by requesting a demonstration in my court. As King of Judea, he comes under my rule. After all, he is from

Nazareth, near Galilee and under my rule. Let him come before his king. He will submit to my will."

Pilate realized that delaying to tell the king was a mistake. He thought it ironic that he defended the prophet man from Herod's anger and frustration. He downplayed the rabbi's provocative behavior earlier, but his disturbance at the temple and conflicts with the Pharisees had raised too many questions. He knew from the reports of Paul what the rabbi could do. He was not like other prophets and, in fact, Pilate believed Jeshua could be unique among men. Another chance to meet with the prophet would help him understand more of Jeshua's strange nature and answer the questions he still harbored within himself.

It was not until the next morning that Pilate sent out several centurions to pass the word along the streets that he was looking for Jeshua. He hoped that Jeshua would not have to face the unpredictable mood of the king before he had a chance to speak to him.

Later that day, one centurion returned with news that Jeshua would arrive at the palace in the evening. Pilate was relieved. He did not want King Herod thinking Jeshua had decided to flee Jerusalem.

Two thieves were brought before Pilate, one accused of stealing bread, the other accused of stealing a purse of coins and knifing his victim, leaving him for dead.

He was accustomed to dealing with vagrants and his judgment was usually swift and harsh. A strange feeling came over him and he thought differently about one thief. Unlike before, he wanted to show clemency to the one stealing bread. The bread thief came before him and he asked, "What is your name boy?"

The young boy spoke with his head down. "Jacob."

"Why did you steal the bread, Jacob?" Pilate prodded.

"My mother is sick."

Pilate interrupted him. "Do not lie to me, boy."

"I was hungry. The smell of the aiish made my belly ache, so I took some, stuffed them into my garebia, and ran as fast as I could."

Pilate waited and then replied. "You are fortunate. I usually cut off the hands of thieves for less. However, today I will reward you for telling me the truth. I will set you free but you must find another way to feed yourself, or else I will have cause to resort to my original intention. Do you understand?"

"You are very kind procurator."

"Do you have a mother, Jacob? If so, I would find her and tell her of your good fortune today."

"Yes, Procurator. My mother lives just outside the city walls. I have not been at my home in two years. She will be happy to see me."

As the boy was about to leave him, Pilate called out to Jacob. "There is a station of food stores below, near the garrison. Tell them I said to give you a week of food for your family."

"You are most kind, Procurator. Thank you...and bless you."

Pilate commanded the centurion to bring in the next thief.

"The rabbi is here. Do you want to see him now?"

"By the gods, yes," Pilate replied. "Send him in and put the second thief in prison. I will deal with him later."

"By your command."

Jeshua entered to see Pilate pouring two cups of wine.

"Please..." Pilate gestured with his hand. "Come in, rabbi. Once again we meet. It is auspicious that we have a chance to speak before the king would have his audience with you."

Jeshua sat opposite Pilate as he offered a cup of wine. "I want to understand the conflict that stands between you and the Sanhedrin. Tell me rabbi, why do they rebuke you? Are you not a Jew and a rabbi?"

"It is true I am a Jew. I have come on behalf of the Father to hold out the truth to all... Jew and Gentile alike. My brethren are not so quick to allow Gentiles the same favor under the house of the Father. The law is very specific. Gentiles are not keen on circumcision and their appetites, of course, run differently."

"Can you tell me more about this Father you speak of? I find it curious that you refer to him as a deity of familial reference. This is most unusual."

"The Father cradles you at birth and at death. He is the maker of all things in heaven and earth. There is nothing you possess, or hope to possess, that does not belong to Him first. Even your position in Judea was destined from the beginning. You must abide by His will and accept it as your own," said Jeshua.

"As the Father's voice, do you have full dominion?"

"I am allowed to express His will for a time, for the purpose of reaching out to men of all nations to repent their pride, arrogance, fear, and greed. Let those that have eyes to see and ears to hear surrender to the Father. Then all things will come to those who will abide. That is His promise.

"In our history, the law of Moses kept my people from straying too far, but now it becomes clear that the law carved into stone cannot account for the changes needed in order to inherit the Father's kingdom. The way is a living way, which stone law cannot abide."

Pilate said, "I do not pretend to know of your laws but I have heard the priests speak of the laws of Moses. Are these the laws you wish to change?"

"These laws can be preserved, I do not come to break them, but rather to offer something higher in principle."

Pilate could not resist asking about what happened at Bethany. "These powers you possess, do they come from your God?"

Jeshua said, "Of these powers you speak, they are not powers as you would know them. No man has any power. Not even Caesar wields any power that the Father does not grant him. The truth is that there is no power, only cooperation, and the wisdom to wield it. You cannot possess power but you can cooperate with life for higher purposes.

"If you try to wield power and control, all that you will do is diminish yourself, and worse, you'll become a sorcerer."

"But have they not declared you to be a sorcerer. Even your own people distrust you. I have heard that the Nazarenes have rejected you and thrown stones. What do you say to this?"

"It is difficult to overcome ignorance. It is often said that a man cannot rise above his familial ties or his community. I do not bring peace to the family or the community. I bring the sword."

Pilate winced and held back his response. Jeshua continued, "If a man shall have life then I invite him to cleave from the mother, to cleave from the father, and even from his children. I shall make them as enemies.

"To them in Nazareth I am not the One, the Messiah, come to give them life, but merely a carpenter's son. Is it not true that in order to rise within your ranks, you have to fight a battle beyond your homeland and then return home triumphant?"

"Are you sure you are not a Roman in disguise?" Pilate chuckled. "How do you hope to change men's hearts, to give them faith in something they cannot see, touch, or taste? They are interested in what fills their bellies and lies only before their noses, otherwise they live in fear that their God will strike them down unless they follow the laws. This is not so different from our Pax Romano or Roman peace. It is only about obedience."

"A loving father expects obedience from his children when they are wayward and troublesome. How much is it unlike this than with the Father who is in heaven, as his children are led astray?"

Pilate had more questions than he started with. He realized he needed more time with the rabbi. He also knew that time was nigh and he must deliver him to Herod.

"Rabbi, I heard you speak of a man's spirit. I have often thought it lives separately, beyond the body and even beyond death. Is a man's death final? I have considered this many times on the battlefield, but never spoken to any man before now. We cannot see this before our eyes. The door is closed to us. Is there life beyond death?"

Jeshua gazed at Pilate fondly. "You have wisdom that belongs from another time. It now calls. The Father has revealed this to you. Among many, you are blessed. The way lives in your heart as God makes his light shine within you, Roman.

"It is said that the way of the heathen leads to Sheol, what we call the grave. Yet I say, if a man allows the light of God to shine within his heart without fear, no grave shall call on the spirit that has awakened."

Pilate got up and took Jeshua's cup. "The time has come for you to see the king. Are you ready?"

Jeshua stood and nodded to Pilate.

They left his quarters together. Pilate ushered Jeshua toward the throne room where King Herod awaited their imminent arrival.

In Herod's Court

Herod was busy entertaining his senatorial friends from Rome when the rabbi and Pilate walked into the throne room. Their entry brought the whole court into silence. Herod expressed a broad smile as though he had just received tribute from one of his rich constituents.

"Procurator, I see you have found the rabbi. We have been so eager to meet you. Word of your reputation precedes your arrival," Herod announced. "We know that you are a rabbi, and have proclaimed yourself to be a prophet as well. So tell us, what is this good news you bring to Judea?"

Jeshua remained quiet.

Herod was not used to having his questions ignored. He started again by cloaking his frustration with humor. "Perhaps the rabbi's voice is vacant because of thirst. Have the desert vultures captured your tongue?" There was brief laughter from the courtesans. "Bring him some of our wine, so that he may speak to us more easily."

He spoke. "I have come to proclaim that God, the Father is now on the earth with love to usher in a new way, his way, a new life that is for all men, Jews and Gentiles alike."

Jeshua starred at the stone floor while he answered Herod. At first, this was taken to be a sign of respect on the rabbi's part, but King Herod sensed his rebellious attitude right away. Pilate realized this meeting was not going to go very well.

"Are you the reincarnation of John the Baptist?" Herod exclaimed with fear.

Jeshua looked up and smiled. "No."

"Are you the Messiah spoken of by the old prophets?"

"Lo, I am the voice of the one true God," said Jeshua. "I am that I am, come to fulfill the law."

Herod wasted no time to strike the next question. "They tell me you are the new King of the Jews. Do you make such a claim before me, King of Judea?"

Jeshua looked at him again. "I have not said this. Others have said it before me. My kingdom does not exist here."

"And where exactly is this kingdom of yours?"

"It is not of this world. It is my Father's kingdom in Heaven, where I shall sit on his right side and rule."

Herod laughed at this but he would not let it go. "Are you the King of the Jews? The Jews do not live in this heaven of yours. They live in this world of Judea where it is that I rule as king." He became agitated. "You speak in riddles, rabbi, like the tongue of a viper. They also tell me that you possess the power to raise the dead. Centurion, draw your sword and plunge it into that man's heart."

Herod pointed to a man standing nearby. The man drew a gasp of air as he saw that his life hung in the moment's imbalance. The soldiers approached the man and King Herod smiled. "Let him demonstrate to us the extent of his power."

Jeshua spoke quickly. "To kill this man is useless, for I will not show the true might of my Father's will to a heathen like yourself for the sake of his pleasure."

Herod held up his hand. "Hold!" The centurion stopped short, much to the relief of the threatened man. "Perhaps this is too large a task for our rabbi to perform today. Indulge me and walk across that pool of water, as you have supposedly done on the Sea of Galilee."

Jeshua shook his head. "I shall not defile the righteousness of my Father to please the whimsical demands of a foolish king."

"We see that you have neither the power to levitate or raise men from the dead. You have disappointed and insulted us. We shall forgive you this time for these indiscretions against your king. This rabbi is a charlatan, a simple liar. These stories are mere fabrications of the foolish people who would follow him. Pilate, take this fraud and get him out of my sight."

Pilate quickly ushered the rabbi from the throne room. "Jeshua, leave here while the king feels magnanimous. This could have gone very bad for you."

"You fear for no reason, Procurator."

Outside the palace, Timothy, James, and John awaited to join him. Pilate watched as they entered the streets and disappeared into the crowds. He was aware of being strangely protective of the rabbi, much to his disbelief. Pilate went back to his quarters and sloshed down ample amounts of wine to sooth his nerves.

"Centurion," he called. "Bring me that thief at once."

When the thief arrived and stood before him, Pilate was already angry. He displaced his anger toward him because the prophet had made him confused. Yet the facts remained that the thief did commit a heinous crime and must be dealt with accordingly.

"You are charged with thievery and stabbing a man to death. By Roman law, your judgment shall be death. Before you die you will be given fifty marks of the lash in the public square, and then taken beyond the gates of the city. There you will be drawn and quartered tomorrow by midday and your remains given to the vultures. Centurion, take this wretched creature from my sight. He disgusts me."

After the thief was led away, Pilate was empty inside. Passing judgment had always made him feel good, as he had rid the world of one less parasite. But now there was an emptiness that he could not shake from his spirit.

Pilate decided to drown in a bit more wine until he passed out. By morning, the day would be as a nightmare that he could easily dismiss and cast out of his mind.

The Warning

Why am I nervous and agitated? Can it be that this man, this prophet, disturbs me so? I have many questions that I believe only he can answer. His words roll around in my mind like unbalanced chariot wheels. I want to put them to rest but I cannot. I want to know more. I fear I shall not sleep until this thirst that wine cannot quench is satisfied. Perhaps I have been bewitched like so many others that come into contact with him. Who is this strange man and why does he affect me so? I must find out, I must know more. Perhaps I will be the one that seeks him out next time.

For now I must get my mind into focus.

***

A week passed. Pilate was unaware that King Herod continued to fester with fears about the rabbi. The king was haunted day and night by his punishment of the Baptist. A strange madness entered his mind. He summoned Pilate to court one evening to confide his deepest fears.

"Pilate, I cannot get the rabbi out of my mind. There is something about the man that reminds me of the Baptist. Do you think that in some demonic way he is the Baptist returned from the dead?"

Pilate interrupted King Herod. "How could that be? I watched as the centurions cleaved his head from his body and buried the remains in the desert. There is no way that is possible."

"What if he has returned to haunt me and torment me for the terrible things I've done? Herodias sleeps as a baby. Nothing seems to trouble her."

"The rabbi and the Baptist shared a common ground in religious ideas as both are Jews. However, it seemed to me they were rivals. I hardly think that one could possess the other. I am no expert in such matters, yet I cannot believe that the rabbi would or could do that. It seems unholy."

"I do not trust him. His people throw stones at him and his followers. I believe he is a false prophet. Unlike the Baptist, I do not believe he is the Messiah."

Herod's confidence in Pilate was fortuitous. Jeshua's provocative demeanor more than frustrated the king. Pilate was surprised that the king did not lash out at him with the fury he had seen him unleash on others.

In the Baptist's case, he lived only because the king genuinely liked him. He fed the king a curious desire to repent for breaking Jewish law. Herod had a different feeling with the prophet, an antagonism, and a desire to move more actively toward eliminating him altogether.

Time was growing short for Jeshua. He was not aware of the impending threat from the king's court. Indeed, he was fortunate the Sanhedrin sided with him for the moment. Pilate knew that his options would narrow to nothing without assistance and wanted to warn him of the forces working against him.

Herod would have Pilate standing by, so any attempts to find the prophet would be, by necessity, more formal than he would like. Pilate needed to create a diversion and give the appearance that he acted on behalf of the king without causing the prophet to distrust his intentions. Pilate decided to seek the man called Peter. Through him, he could let the prophet know of his intention to meet privately and on friendly terms.

***

On the eve of the next day, Pilate set out to find Peter. Three separate contacts gave him wrong places to look. On the fourth try, he learned that Peter was near the Gethsemane grotto speaking about the differences between the old laws of Moses and the new approach ascribed to Jeshua. When Pilate arrived, he heard Peter say, "It is said in the old law a man must pay equal to his trespass against his neighbor, but the Master says if a man demands a coat from you then give him your shirt also."

The small crowd exchanged with each other until a listener chimed in, "Simon, what if someone takes you to court over a disagreement about an exchange of goods. What should you do?"

"The Master says better to settle your affairs before it goes to the court, for then you are liable and subject to the suitor and the court," said Peter.

The crowd argued among themselves until another called out, "Teacher, what should a man do if a woman is tired of her husband and no longer wishes to be bound by her marriage vows to him because she finds another man more worthy?"

"The law says that no man can undo the vow of marriage, lest both of you commit adultery. This is true for a man who no longer seeks his wife, or the woman who seeks another man, but I tell you that the Master says, if you are coveting after another outside of your marriage vows then you are already committing adultery in your heart. It is better that you relinquish the marriage and find cause for annulling the vows, than to continue to dishonor the vows before God in your heart one after another."

The Warning **143**

The crowd grumbled and said that Peter blasphemed and sinned for teaching a false doctrine. Some picked up rocks and threw them at him. They continued to yell until Pilate stepped in and drew his sword, threatening that they should disperse before he had them arrested. The crowd began to scatter, afraid that the Romans would put them in prison. After they were gone, Pilate took the opportunity to approach Peter.

"You, the one they call Simon the fisherman, are you alright?"

Peter responded nervously. "Yes. I have done nothing wrong. What do you want with me?"

"You speak very abruptly to one who has just saved your life," said Pilate. "Do not be alarmed. I have come to give you a message for your Master, the rabbi."

Peter was suspicious as he wiped blood from his forehead where a rock had met its mark. "Are you not Pilate, the Procurator? How very strange that the Roman Procurator of Judea would protect a follower of the rabbi. Even stranger, he wants to give a message to Jeshua. What strange business is this? Why would Rome take such a personal interest in our rabbi?"

"We mean him no harm. On the contrary, I have an urgent message, a warning really. I came myself because contact with him by others would become dangerous for both of our sakes. I thought it better coming from you than from me."

Peter grew intrigued by Pilate's concern. "What is so urgent, Roman?"

"Your rabbi is in danger," Pilate said.

"In danger? In what way?"

"Believe me, fisherman, when I say he must be very careful. King Herod is very upset. He wants harm to come to Jeshua."

"But he has just returned from court. The king found no serious fault with him."

"The king has asked that I take his case to the High Counsel and the High Priest. I tell you, the king is plotting against him. He is trying to build a case against him. Herod knows that the Sanhedrin, the Sadducees, and the Pharisees favor him right now, and he wants to change that. The king intends to apply political pressure. I believe you are all in danger here in Jerusalem."

Peter accepted the warning as real. "The Master has gone back to Galilee and we cannot reach him before morning. I will tell him what you have said. Thank you for your kindness, brother from Rome. We are in your debt."

Peter placed his hand on Pilate's shoulder as though they were old friends. Pilate bid him good journey and left. He rode to the palace, pondering his

The Warning 145

unbelievable actions. He had become a conspirator with the rabbi and his followers. The situation for Pilate was remarkable and frightening.

Peter returned to the inn where he was staying and told James the Just and John what Pilate had said. James expressed doubt about the Procurator's good gesture. Peter said that he believed him, and that he had saved him from a stoning by the angry crowd as proof of his good will. James was glad that Peter came to no harm, though he was troubled about being in debt to Pilate. He remained skeptical but agreed they should tell Jeshua at once.

Within the hour, Peter, James, and John left to join Jeshua in Galilee. They gathered their slings and traveled through the night, and reached their destination by morning.

James spoke first to Jeshua. "Master, we come with urgent news from Jerusalem. According to the procurator, Pontius Pilate, the king has begun to plot against us in the Sanhedrin."

"Pilate said this himself?" asked Jeshua.

"Yes, Master," said Peter. "I for one believe him."

"This is interesting. Rome and our mission have become strange bedfellows. I suspected that Pilate was sympathetic, but not to this degree."

"Master, it is no longer safe to openly preach in Jerusalem," said James. "If you will forgive my saying so, this is no time for the lady, especially in her condition, to be with us."

Jeshua became pensive. "I suppose you are right. Mary needs to go where she can birth safely out of harm's way. There are difficult times ahead."

He sat on a stone impediment and folded his arms. For a short time, he said nothing. He placed his face in his hands as though he was in deep pain. James approached to console him, but stopped when Jeshua brought both hands smartly on his lap. He smiled and slapped his legs as his followers looked on with confusion. Jeshua said, "James, I want you and John to take Mary to Ephases, in Phrygia near the Black Sea. I have friends there to care for her until I call for her. Peter and I will return to Jerusalem."

Jeshua joined Mary in the room where she sat combing her red hair. He was preoccupied and displayed a furrowed brow. "What is it, my love? You look upset."

"Conditions in Jerusalem have taken a darker turn, Mary. It is necessary that we get you to safety."

"Absolutely not. I will remain with you no matter what happens."

"It will soon become impossible to move you safely without compromising our position. We must take you to a place where you can birth without worry for the welfare of the child."

"I have seen women drop their babies in the middle of the desert without a second thought and then continue on. I am not different from them and I am stronger than I look." She smiled at him. "I want to stay with you, my love, under any circumstances. Besides, I want you there when the child comes."

"I know the strength of your stubbornness as well as your other admirable strengths, but like it or not, you will be a distraction at this critical time. Things are well in hand. I want you to focus on the child and leave these matters to me."

Mary saw that Jeshua had made up his mind. She knew that he could be as stubborn as she and he was not going to move from his position. Mary reluctantly yielded.

At sunrise the next day, they parted. Jeshua headed back to Jerusalem with Peter while Mary, James, and John began the long journey to Phrygia.

Meanwhile, inside Jerusalem, Simon the Zealot joined with other zealots in the vast catacombs beneath the city. Their agenda to assault the Romans had not subsided from their failure at the Great Temple. Many of their friends were dead or in prison, including Barabbas, one of the leaders of the rebellion. Simon, disappointed that Jeshua did not come to their aid, had not given up on his support of their cause. He had heard the Master talk of the sword on many occasions and convinced the remaining band of rebels that Jeshua would join them under the right conditions.

Then Simon said that he heard from Peter. Mary, almost at full term with child, was traveling to Phrygia and this presented a wonderful opportunity. Simon had a plan on how to inspire Jeshua to attack the Romans. Zealots would follow Mary and kill her and the child, and blame the attack on the Romans. He believed Jeshua would surely rise with hunger for revenge. The zealots agreed and sent two assassins, Zebadai and Ethias, to find her.

They knew that James and John were on foot and Mary rode a donkey. Having already traveled for two days on their journey, Zebadai and Ethias went on camels to make up the lost time.

John arranged for passage across the Aegean Sea by small ship. Zebadai and Ethias wanted to reach them before they set sail, but a terrible sand storm delayed them. They arrived at the port too late.

***

Three weeks later, the zealots arrived in Bithynia. As their camels lowered to the kneeling position, they saw a pregnant woman near the well. Mary waited with John while James negotiated for camels to continue their journey. Ethias recognized John from the day at the Great Temple. The woman must be Mary. He looked at Zebadai and signaled that he had found their target.

Zebadai dismounted his camel and Ethias offered to pull water from the well for Mary so she might be cooled from the heat. She nodded yes to his kindness and turned her back to him as she called out to John, "Do you want a drink of water?"

As John turned Ethias grabbed her from behind. He struggled to hold her and pulled a sword from his robe to cut her throat. Mary broke away. He managed one swipe of his sword against her arm and her flesh fell open to splatter blood against the well. She went down as John leaped over the well to block the next thrust of Ethias' sword toward her belly.

Zebadai rushed in to assist in the slaughter and attacked John with a severe cut to the shoulder and brought him down on one knee. As Zebadai raised his sword to behead him, James appeared from behind and thrust his sword into Zebadai's back, reaching his heart. Zebadai fell dead. John grew faint from his wound and through the haze saw Mary on the ground as Ethias stood over her.

Ethias paused when his ally fell to the ground dead and recommitted himself to the cause of killing Mary. Ethias made another swing at Mary's neck but John made a last conscious effort and lunged with his sword to block Ethias from his mortal blow. This gave time for James to arrive and cleave the zealot's head from his body. The head flew into the well as the body dropped lifeless before Mary. She bled profusely and joined John in unconsciousness, leaving James the only one standing.

James sought refuge in a nearby inn so he could tend to their wounds. The zealots did not succeed in killing Mary, but her water broke in the deadly skirmish. She carried twin boys who were born dead. They stayed in Bithynia for several weeks to heal from their wounds before they pushed on to Phrygia.

Mary was devastated. While she stayed in Phrygia, she had a deep sadness for her loss. James stayed with her while John returned to Jerusalem to tell Jeshua of their terrible experience.

Simon the Zealot had failed. Jeshua was angry with the zealots and their plot against him. His intention to have Jeshua blame the Romans for their loss was lost in the deaths of his sons. Jeshua suspected Simon's complicity, and Simon kept silent about his part in hopes there would be another chance to overthrow the Roman occupation.

The Last Stand

When an officer is on the battlefield and he senses enemy forces are building on his flanks, his choices for a good strategy become dangerously narrow. After years of battle experience, such an officer, if he is a good officer, develops a peculiar hunch. He learns quickly to rely on such urges. When I returned to my quarters, I could not shake the feeling that Jerusalem would be the place where I would make my final stand, to confirm well-earned laurels of a fine military career or descend quickly into disgrace and dishonor.

When I took that awful step to warn the rabbi, I realized that my fate was tied irrevocably to his. My option to remain neutral in this matter has closed, leaving me with a need to be cautious in my actions.

As governor, there were always duties of office that kept me busy, but my heart was distant and unenthusiastic. I drank more over the next weeks as the Jewish Passover celebration quickly approached. Emotions always ran high during this time. The crowds became unruly and more distressed about their troubles, especially concerning the Roman *occupation.*

I hoped for news about the prophet man, but no word of his whereabouts came to me. One morning I overheard members of the High Counsel talk openly that Jeshua, the renegade priest, planned to attend a special meeting with Caiaphas and the Counsel within the next few days. I was excited at the possibility of another meeting with the prophet. I had many more questions and my assistance to him should offer me the possibility for another private audience. I learned of rumors about his misfortune regarding the attacks on his wife and two of his closest followers. These were terrible times and the path he walked was fraught with danger and treachery.

There had been no pomp or glory in his entry into Jerusalem this time. He entered the city like a thief. No crowds gathered around him and his visit to the Great Temple occurred in the middle of the night. The High Counsel met with him in secrecy. I would not have known about his appearance except that the Temple soldiers related the news to my guards.

***

Caiaphas made sure that not all seventy of the priesthood was present when the prophet arrived. The key members of the High Counsel included

Nicodemus, Joseph of Arimathea, Levi, Ethanea, Ishmael, Bathsuha, and Caiaphas. They formed into a semicircle so that they could make eye contact with each other during the interview.

The prophet entered into the darkened chamber with his hands clasped in front of him. Priests of the higher Sanhedrin often displayed this respectful posture. This was a subtle sign to the others that he saw himself as equal, if not greater, than they were. It was a challenge to their authority as keepers of the law.

He did not address them from a position of subordination. The tone of the interview placed Jeshua as judge before the High Counsel instead of the other way around.

Levi fired the first question. "By what authority do you have to come before this Counsel with such a posture?"

Jeshua answered, "By what authority do you have the right to question my posture?"

Ethanea spoke next. "Ours is granted through the great lineage of the Sadducees and Pharisees, established by the first Sanhedrin and called forth by the Lord God the Father. But we have not heard testimony regarding your authority, Rabbi."

"I have been charged by my Father in Heaven to speak for him in his stead."

Bathsuha spoke to the rabbi. "Are you saying that you are the embodiment of the law? By the very words you speak, through this false oral doctrine, you are breaking the law."

"The Lord God spews the law from His mouth and it is through Him, made manifest in me. I am here before you to fulfill that law, not to break the law."

The group arose and began to shake their fists at Jeshua. They proclaimed that he sinned against the law in speaking as the almighty sovereign God.

Caiaphas raised his hands for quiet. "Brothers please...perhaps it is that we rush to judgment and find fault where there may be only confusion from his words. Let us calm down and let the rabbi speak to us."

The priests sat back down, still grumbling among themselves.

Caiaphas asked, "Tell us Rabbi, why do you believe the oral tradition you bring has greater validity than that handed down from Moses?"

Jeshua stood pensive for a moment. "Is it not true before Moses wrote down the laws that God gave to him to bring to his people, God began an oral tradition. He did not write that Moses should go and tell the Pharaoh to let his people go, He spoke those words to Moses directly. Did not God tell Moses to release the plagues on the people of Egypt if they did not comply, so they would know the power of the one true God?"

Nicodemus addressed the rabbi. "You speak as if you know God and what he thinks. How is this possible?"

"What is the most important law?" asked Jeshua.

"To love the Lord God with all your heart, mind, and body, and to keep the Sabbath holy."

Jeshua looked at Nicodemus with great compassion and tears came to his eyes. "Nicodemus, your understanding is great and I tell you on this day, your heart does not lie far from the Father's kingdom. Therefore, you shall reside in my Father's house forever."

A flush of heat rushed into the chamber. The room was suddenly silent. All eyes turned from Nicodemus and back to Caiaphas. The priests were helpless. It seemed to be a stalemate.

Caiaphas released their anguish. "We are not displeased with your eloquence on the scripture. No one has brought more life into the holy words for the people to hear in a very long time. You have returned the faithful to the law. We are encouraged by your passion but some of your statements greatly trouble us. You say you do not come to break the law yet you stand here and defy the law by proclaiming to be God's mouthpiece. I ask you plainly, are you the

Messiah?"

Jeshua did not answer.

Caiaphas asked, "Is it true that you are the King of the Jews?"

Again, Jeshua said nothing.

Joseph of Arimethea asked of Jeshua, "Master, when you healed the sick and cast out devils, in what name did you do these things?"

"Brother Joseph," said Jeshua smiling. "It is not for me that I do these things but for my Father in heaven. These tasks are to show the power of His love and compassion for man. I am but a vessel by which His power and glory is manifest upon the earth."

Joseph turned to the rest. "There do you not see, brothers? He has a good heart and means no harm. He is a teacher, a prophet, and I for one believe that he is the One, and come to set the way for us. You have to but open your hearts and see the truth of it. The Messiah stands before us."

Caiaphas turned to Joseph. "You have always had an admiration for those who are passionate. Perhaps you and Nicodemus will stay a while longer. The rest can go. We will deliberate further before we make our decision."

Levi and the others left the chamber, and Caiaphas turned to Jeshua. "Come sit, Rabbi. Let us drink tea and talk of this doctrine of yours."

For hours, the four priests discussed various aspects of the law and Jeshua's doctrine. At the end, Caiaphas concluded, as did Nicodemus, there were no complaints to be made about the young rabbi's doctrinal interpretations. Joseph all but declared his discipleship to Jeshua, and Nicodemus was not far from supporting Jeshua as well. Even Caiaphas was duly impressed and wanted to know more.

Caiaphas shared his concerns regarding King Herod. "Rabbi, you must be cautious with the king. He disfavors you in ways I do not understand. It is better that you stay out of his way. He might become a serious problem for your ministry in Jerusalem. He does not trust you and has already said so to the Counsel. We will reassure him of your good will."

Jeshua responded, "You overestimate the king's capacities. There is little that he can do."

"There is much he can do. He can override our influence and have you crucified," said Caiaphas.

"Herod would not dare to crucify the Messiah," Jeshua declared.

"You underestimate his power. His friends in the Roman Senate extend all the way to the Emperor."

"Do not be afraid. God's will shall prevail on earth and no earthly kingdom shall have dominion over Him."

Caiaphas was shocked at the arrogance of Jeshua,

but he realized that his purpose represented an aspect of Divine Will. He decided to yield to Jeshua for now.

When Jeshua left the Great Temple, he met John and James and retreated to the garden of Gethsemane not far from the city. Jeshua said that they would make camp so he could spend time to meditate. John and James fell asleep while Jeshua sat in deep contemplation. He heard a voice that sounded familiar. Jeshua opened his eyes to see a mist form in front of him and gathering light.

"Jeshua, Jeshua. I am come into your midst once again," the angel said.

"Who are you, angel, and do you bring tidings from my Father?"

"I am Melchizedek and I bring great tidings. Your Father loves you, Jeshua, and your task on Earth is almost over. Yet, there is still another task you must do. It is the will of the Lord God that His force and light be withdrawn from you. You are to be as the lamb brought to a slaughter, for His sake."

Jeshua dropped to his knees. "But why? Have I not pleased Him? Am I being punished?"

Melchizedek placed his hand on the head of Jeshua and a great light and heat rose from his body. He declared, "You are now merely a man and no longer bear the Christ force within. It is important that you complete this last task as a man."

"Father, Father, why have you forsaken me? Angel, tell me what my Father wants of me."

Melchizedek took pity on Jeshua. In the pain and loss of God's presence, the angel revealed his future.

"Behold." Melchizedek waved his hand in front of Jeshua and in the air before him, he saw what God had planned. He saw himself betrayed by Judas and his closest friends denying they knew him. He saw himself captured, beaten, and tortured with a thorny crown, humiliated and laughed at, and then saw himself crucified on a tree dying alone with no one there to console him.

Jeshua fell to the ground sobbing. "Why me, Lord? Why must I suffer?"

Melchizedek dissolved and a golden light shone on Jeshua.

"Why do you lament? Have I not honored you by giving you My vital force to do with as you wanted? You must understand now, that it is not only important for you to reveal My will and presence upon the earth at this time, it becomes important that one is chosen, who through faith and spiritual work, inherits my heart, but then through that redemption must show the way for all others to see the truth about their fall from grace and the way back, which is through their suffering for their righteous indignation and pride, and then

they shall earn their grace again."

Jeshua rose from the ground and placed his hands in a prayer. Tears streamed from his eyes. "Father, please pass this cup from me."

In a few moments the light that surrounded him faded. Jeshua knew, as he thought to himself, "Not my will, Father, but Your will be done."

Judas' Betrayal

I was shocked to learn of Paul's intentions in this affair, but after considering his position in Rome, it began to make perfect sense. His shrewdness he learned from the masters of shrewdnes. Perhaps those who had invented shrewdness were in the senate of Rome.

In my years as a military officer, I have watched in awe as those who wielded political favors for personal gain built their personal empires within the empire. I also watched those who were not as clever at the game get swept away beneath the feet of those who were more clever. I feared for the rabbi. Though I did not know him well, he did not seem to understand the art and finesse of political maneuvering as I did.

***

As Jeshua met with the High Counsel in Jerusalem, Paul was busy making contact with a close friend and member of the Roman Senate, Gaius Macenius. He told Gaius that he had infiltrated the group following the renegade rabbi called Jeshua.

Before Paul could tell Gaius his plan to undermine the rabbi, Gaius informed him that Emperor Tiberius already knew about Jeshua from complaints by King Herod.

The king's reaction to Jeshua had created a strong negative response from the Emperor. Tiberius told Herod that he should do everything in his power to crush the rebellion of this rabbi. The king would otherwise lose the promised future support from Rome toward expanding his rule to the other provinces of Judea.

With Rome's support, Herod could apply pressure to the Sanhedrin to bring charges against the rabbi. Paul realized the opportunity to meld his own plan with the Emperor's edict. He sought to have another ally assist him to accelerate the rabbi's undoing. Paul thought of a young scribe in Rome named Judas Iscariot. He would suggest to Jeshua to accept him as a disciple.

Paul was politically astute and read the signs of Rome's decline. The difficulties of maintaining rule in the foreign provinces required a constant increase of military strength to fortify the borders, and left Rome at risk. There was also intrigue and unrest within the Senate, and Paul saw that Tiberius was the last of the great emperors. It would only be a matter of time before the strength of the Republic suffered with the decline of the Emperor, as Tiberius was not getting any younger.

Nero was next in line. This was common knowledge among the power elite and all knew no good would come of it. There were constant rumors of senatorial power and influence waning, and the republic leaning towards dictatorship. These were turbulent times for the Empire.

Paul dreamed of rising to greater influence and personal dignity. Rome loomed far too close to instability and treachery for his taste. He saw a possibility with this new movement. The newly formed religion known as the Christian movement was perfect for him if handled in the right way. His leadership and skill with politics could confirm its successful integration into Rome. The old gods were losing favor with the people. Paul saw Christianity as the new religion of Rome, and would ensure his legacy and return to the center of the Empire.

Jeshua stood in his way. If he eliminated the rabbi, only Peter, James, and John might inhibit his plan further. They were ignorant men and not much to consider, but they were devoted to the Master.

Paul had to convince Emperor Tiberius that the best way to control the rebellion was to replace the renegade priest with one that favored Rome, and then lead the followers astray. Paul could shape the chaos for his own advantage.

***

Paul brought Judas Iscariot to the camp of Jeshua. He encouraged him to be bold and introduce himself. Jeshua sat near the fire with his back snugly against a small olive tree. His eyes were closed in deep meditation and he did not hear Judas approach.

"Master," he called softly. "Master, my name is Judas, Judas Iscariot. I have heard so much about you. I want to follow you and learn from you."

Jeshua looked up. "What did you say your name was?"

"Judas, Master."

Jeshua fell hard on the vision that Melchizedek revealed. The face of Judas rolled in front of him. His eyes opened wide to embrace the fate that sat in front of him. He had arrived sooner than he anticipated. Jeshua dropped his head as fear filled his heart. His heartbeat slowed from the rapid flutter of a bird's wing to a dull groan. The cold desert night wrapped around him like a clench of inescapable death.

This confrontation with his fate culminated in absolute despair. Jeshua no longer commanded his own destiny. All he could do was agree. He grinned at the irony of the situation and said, "Yes, you may

Judas' Betrayal   165

follow me."

Judas smiled. Even he did not suspect his true role in meeting the rabbi. Paul had not told Judas about the true purpose for him joining the small band of disciples.

"This is wonderful, Master. You have made me happy. I have many skills that I will use to serve you."

Jeshua leaned back against the tree and closed his eyes. "I am tired. Let me sleep." He said within his mind one more lament, *"Father, why must you hasten my undoing within hardly another breath?"*

Judas retreated to the fire. A piece of lamb clung to a stick hanging over the fire. He took from it a small morsel and began chewing. He sat quietly, pleased with himself.

On the evening of the second night, Jeshua secured rooms at one of the inns inside the city. He anticipated the arrival of James and John with Mary. Jeshua was grateful for their safe return. He embraced his wife warmly and she wept as she told him of their loss and narrow escape from death.

Jeshua sobbed with her. She did not know of his deeper feelings of helplessness that went through his heart. He could not bring himself to tell her what had happened with Melchizedek. Her pain was deep enough. He consoled her with the hope of a better future. Jeshua shared his deepest gratitude to James and John for their valiant efforts to ward off the danger they encountered. He retreated with Mary into their room for the night.

Five days before the festival of Passover, Paul took Judas aside. He influenced Judas through negative innuendo, and slowly set Judas against Jeshua by creating doubt. It was excellent timing. Judas had not yet formed any strong opinions or close associations with the other disciples.

Paul knew that the others vied for Jeshua's attention and they were slow to accept new members. Paul's tutelage made Judas a perfect scapegoat. He had joined the group with great enthusiasm and dedication to the Master, which ensured an instant irritation. This kept him isolated and open to further influence by Paul. Judas was an intelligent man but ignorant of such clever maneuvering. He looked at Paul as a mentor. Not once did he suspect Paul's true intentions.

Judas loved to hear Jeshua speak of God and the inner workings of man's spirit. Much to the annoyance of the others, he was quick to ask questions on every subject as it came up. Paul believed that Jeshua had begun to like Judas.

Paul did not know that Jeshua was aware of Judas' true purpose. He made an extra effort to ward off the effect of Jeshua's affection because Paul knew how strong that influence would undermine what he wanted to accomplish.

The night of Passover arrived. Jeshua planned a special gathering for the evening. He explained that he had important news and asked the innkeeper to set aside a table in the rear of the inn where they could enjoy privacy. John and James sat on one side next to Thomas, while Paul, Mary, and Peter sat on the other side of Jeshua. Judas sat across the table from Jeshua.

Several loaves of unleavened bread were piled in a large wooden bowl in the middle of the table. Wine drawn from a large barrel filled a large clay pitcher fitted with two long looping handles, and was near the bread. Each disciple had a small earthen plate and shallow clay cup. Though they could hold the cup by one hand, it was easier to use both.

Music came from camelhair bows that dragged melodic hypnotic drones from stringed koras, and small drums shook with jangling cymbals to play out local rhythms. Merriment roared back to the little hovel in the rear, helping to fill in the long pauses that drifted between the disciples.

All were pensive. The air carried an almost threatening current. Mary was sick from the morose feeling and left the gathering for bed. An intermittent evening breeze from the desert wafted through the inn to the back, offering a slight chill that seeped into their hearts and added an unknown anguish. They drank and ate without speaking until the late hours.

Finally Jeshua spoke. He was tired and weary. His weak voice dangled in the air like the song of a night bird. He looked at his friends sorrowfully. "This will be the last time I will break bread with you, my brothers. For soon I will no longer be with you."

Peter grabbed his arm. "Where ever you go, Master, I will follow."

They all agreed, but then Jeshua said, "Where I go you cannot follow."

The disciples cried out, "Where are you going? We want to come with you."

Jeshua bowed his head. "One of you will betray me."

"Master, is it me?" John said.

James asked, "Is it me? You can tell me."

Jeshua said nothing more. Peter leaned over and whispered softly, "Master, I would never betray you. I love you."

Jeshua declared, "Peter, before the cock crows twice tonight, you will deny me three times."

He shook his head in disbelief. Then Jeshua leaned toward him. "Watch, Peter. The one who betrays me will dip his bread into the oil at the same time as I."

Jeshua broke open a loaf of bread and tore a small piece. As he reached for the bowl of oil, Judas also dipped his morsel of bread. Jeshua grabbed his wrist.

"Do what you must, and do it quickly."

Judas was shocked by Jeshua's action. He broke into tears and blurted out, "Why, Lord? Why must it be me?"

Jeshua held him close. He confided in Judas that there was no blame in this. Judas wept that he had come to love Jeshua and though he had doubts, he could not accept the task.

Jeshua comforted him. "As this is your lot to bear, decreed by divine will, so it is my lot to accept that I must suffer. This you must do, my friend, because if you do not, then my purpose for coming here is of no consequence."

The rabbi poured wine into his cup. "Drink your fill if it will help to brace you in this deed."

Judas gulped several cups of wine before he staggered to the door of the inn. He looked back mournfully at Jeshua for one last time and disappeared into the night.

Jeshua turned to the others and broke another piece of bread from a loaf. He said, "Kath-Sume Vau Ah leh Meh Sheude. Let us eat this bread together one last time."

He poured wine into his cup and said, "Tah-Meh-Ish-Vau-Ah-Leh-Meh-Sheude. Let us drink together one last time."

The disciples ate the bread and drank the wine

without understanding the meaning. Jeshua left the table. "John and James, come with me while I meditate in the garden."

Peter said, "Master, I want to come with you, too."

Jeshua nodded in the affirmative.

***

Judas soon appeared at the palace gates. "I know where the rabbi is. I know where he is and I will help you find him." He lost his balance and fell down the steps. Judas began to laugh, and also wept while he laughed. He tried to climb back until the centurions blocked his entry by crossing their spears in front of his face.

"You must let me pass," he cried. "I have knowledge that the king wants."

"You are drunk," one centurion replied. "Go away before we throw you into the dungeon to sleep it off."

"The king will be very angry with you if you do not listen to me. I am one of them, I tell you. I am here to betray him."

The captain of Pilate's personal guard came to the entrance. "You there, centurion, what is cause of the noise?"

"This man is drunk. He claims to be with those Christians and knows where the renegade rabbi hides."

"Let me see him," the captain demanded. "I know this man. I have seen him with the rabbi. They call him Judas." He looked down on Judas. "Can you really tell us where he is, this rabbi of yours, or are you too drunk?"

Judas heaved half-eaten bread mixed with wine on the stones. He wiped his mouth and replied, "I can. May God forgive me, it is my duty."

The captain turned to the centurions. "Call out half the guard. If he is wrong, we won't wake up the neighborhood and look like fools."

Troops assembled at the gates in full armor with Judas in front. Before long, he led them up the path to the olive groves at the outskirts of the city walls.

Jeshua sat waiting inside the garden of Gethsemane. James, John, and Peter lay nearby fast asleep. A small night breeze blew and the deep black night sky hung overhead.

"James and John, you are my closest friends," he whispered. "Can you not stay awake with me in my hour of need? You would leave your Master alone to face his destruction?"

They did not hear him. The sound of tromping feet and metal sheaths brushing hard against leather tunics pounded through the grove of olive trees to the entrance of the garden. The Roman soldiers stopped, and Judas told the captain that he would signal to them which man was the rabbi. He would embrace him with a kiss. Then they could move in and capture him.

Judas entered the garden and went to Jeshua, who he embraced and kissed him on the cheek.

Jeshua was astonished. "So you would betray your Master with a kiss?"

The soldiers rushed in and woke James and John. James drew his sword and lopped off the ear of the first centurion. Other soldiers subdued him with spears and separated James from the rest.

Jeshua cried out, "Stop, James. Those who live by the sword shall die by the sword. Lay down your weapon. There is nothing to be done here. It is finished."

The soldiers escorted Jeshua away in shackles. They pushed and shoved at him while James fell to the ground. John and Peter held him.

James called to Jeshua, "No, wait. Oh no, Master!"

***

In the morning Judas stumbled through the streets of Jerusalem, still drunk and full of grief. He met an old man who limped with a dried branch propped under his arm.

When he saw Judas he said, "Did you hear? They

have arrested the Rabbi Jeshua?"

Judas looked at the man with reddened eyes. "I would not know of this."

Later Judas found himself weaving in front of the Great Temple. Two Sadducees who did not favor the rabbi appeared at the gates and gazed down on Judas with sardonic grins.

"A man who has done his job well deserves to be paid." They tossed a bag with thirty pieces of silver at his feet. "With that prize, you can buy more to drink."

The Trial

I did not learn of the rabbi's capture and arrest until morning. By then I had discovered the treatment he received from my centurions. They brought him in just before daybreak. The initial charge against him was sedition. Normally I would not allow the treatment he received under such circumstances. He had two aspects working against him. First, he was a prophet and no one within the ranks of the Roman military ever favored a prophet. Second, they labeled him a seditionist and that is the worst of all, because that meant he was an enemy of Rome.

The centurions did not know what outcome would befall him from a trial, so they decided to administer the corporal punishment befitting such a criminal. They stripped him of his robes, revealing his naked body. Some circled him and beat him with wooden sticks. Then they tied his hands to his feet with leather straps from a horse's saddle to prevent him from standing. They dragged him through the mud on his side and followed that by dragging him through horse dung. To keep him from crying out, they stuffed his mouth with dung and wrapped it with a cloth.

Afterward they brought him to the third level of the garrison and into a small room where they hooked him over a wooden post that stood in the middle of the floor. There they whipped him bloody while the others watched with demonic pleasure. He collapsed unconscious several times but he was revived with pails of cold water thrown on him.

When I arrived, they were putting the last touch on their handiwork. Someone had fashioned a crown made from the branches of a blackthorn bush. Each of the spines was as long as the spread of three fingers. They laughed at him as the crown was crushed down on his scalp. Blood streamed down his face and into his eyes and mouth from where the thorns penetrated his scalp and brow.

The centurions called out, "Behold, a fitting crown for a king."

One soldier pulled a red cloth used to wrap around urns filled with wine, and draped it over him. "A king cannot go forth without a kingly robe. Behold, the King of the Jews."

As I approached, laughter rang through the dark narrow hall before me. I entered the torch-lit room, and was speechless when the soldiers parted the way for me to reveal the sight of Jeshua. I screamed. They thought I had joined in their merriment until they realized I was serious. The room went quiet as I approached. The rabbi lifted his head to peer from his beaten and swollen eyes that were drenched in blood. I held his head. I did not know if his condition was critical or not. I called for a physician to care for what was left of him.

The captain tried to make excuses for the men. I stopped him with the wave of my hand. If he had uttered one more regrettable word from his mouth, I swear I would have had his tongue removed.

I regretted the deeds done this morning, but there was no reversing them. My harsh reactions confused the men and they feared for their safety from my anger. These actions always arose in such cases and nothing was ever said to countermand them before. Why now? Why with this man?

I cannot explain my feelings, not even to myself. I said to my men, "You have committed wrong. This man has not been charged or gone to trial yet. Clean this place and make it ready for my inspection within the hour."

When a soldier is confused he needs direction to take his mind off the disturbing elements around him. Cleaning details are good for that purpose. Besides, I wanted to get rid of the stench of his spilt blood seeping into the wood floor and walls of that awful room. I fear that my dreams will be forever haunted with the events of this day.

The physician came and cleaned and dressed his wounds. I made sure that the rabbi had his clothing returned to him. I still had to attend to the matter at hand. I cannot erase the fact that an arrest has taken place. I needed to talk with him and this is not the premise I had in mind. I had him brought to my chambers. I poured wine for the rabbi and questioned him.

***

"It is unfortunate the soldiers captured you before I could control the situation. There may have been something I could have done."

"There is nothing you can do for me. It is out of your hands," Jeshua said.

Pilate bowed his head. "I hoped we would get another chance to talk. I have so many questions. Now you stand accused of sedition by Rome and she is thirsty for your inquisition and execution. The Sanhedrin has also turned against you and seized the opportunity to make you an example. I have to put aside all that I wanted and deal with you very differently."

Pilate turned to the balcony and watched the crowds gathering in the square for Passover. He tried to think of anything that could alleviate the situation placed before him. For the first time, he felt regret. If only he could find another to make the decision for him. Pilate had not foreseen this in his career. Then, an epiphany struck him. "By the gods," he called out. "Octavius, come here at once."

His guard entered out of breath. "Yes, Procurator. What is it?"

"Is there not an ancient rule in Jerusalem that clemency can be granted during festivals?"

"Yes, though it has not been summoned in a long time. It is still legal, I believe."

"Send a message to Caiaphas at once. Tell him I wish to evoke the right of an officer of the Roman court to demand clemency from the Sanhedrin for Passover. We cannot call on the king as I suspect he has already passed judgment. Do this quickly. We have little time left to us."

"By your command, Procurator." Octavius sped from the chamber.

Pilate looked at Jeshua. "I know you have given up, and with what you have already suffered, I fully understand, but there is still a chance to turn this around."

Jeshua gave him a sad smile. "You are wasting your time. It is the Will of my Father that my fate is so. You have no power to overturn His Will."

They waited for Octavius to return. "I have news

from the high priest. He said that clemency could only be granted by the will of the people. He can do nothing beyond this to help the rabbi. He said place him before the people along with a condemned prisoner so they can make a fair choice."

Pilate rubbed his chin. This is risky at best, he thought, but perhaps a way out for me as well. If the crowd does not choose him, I have still done my best for the rabbi.

He turned to Octavius. "Prepare an announcement for the people on the precipice by the square and bring Barabbas from his cell. We shall let them decide, the rabbi or Barabbas."

Pilate would easily put his personal feelings aside for the prophet for the sake of his career. This was his opportunity to make amends with the people. He made several mistakes with the people of Palestine. Not only did Rome need to be appeased but the whole of Judea as well.

Guards led Barabbas to the terrace that overlooked the square. Some of the people began to chant Barabbas' name. The guards brought Jeshua and stood him next to the rebel zealot. Soon Pilate appeared before the crowd.

Centurions stood shoulder to shoulder armed with crossbows and spears. No one dared approach too close.

Pilate raised his arms to quiet the crowd. "Friends, as Procurator of Judea I welcome you to this day's festivities. It is the time of your highest religious rituals and celebrations. As Romans, we wish to make an unusual gesture in honor of this holy day. The right afforded to us by ancient decree on high holy celebrations such as this is to grant clemency to one who has been condemned to death. Therefore, I will conduct a ritual of my own."

Servants brought out a bowl of water and placed it inside a stand having three legs. They stood by with a towel awaiting his next cue. Pilate dipped his hands into the bowl of water. "As it is, so that all can see, I wash my hands of the business that stands before us. I take no responsibility for what you choose. The fate of these men rests solely in your hands. Give us your choice. Let a cheer be heard for the rabbi, Jeshua. Do you wish that he be freed?"

There were screams and pleading from within the crowd and jeering from others for Jeshua. Zealots near the women making the most sound in favor of Jeshua knocked them down and kicked them until they could not speak. Mary the Magdalene was punched in the stomach, knocking the breath out of her, and another zealot struck her on the head. She dropped unconscious to the ground. Pilate called out for the crowd to cheer for Barabbas. A roar arose from the crowd, filled with zealot supporters and those who wanted the rabbi punished for his blasphemy.

Pilate lowered his head. "So be it. The zealot Barabbas goes free. Put the rabbi into a cell until his sentence is carried out."

The guards released Barabbas from his shackles. He rubbed his wrists, shocked that he had escaped his death. He shook his fists with joy and hopped off the terrace into the waiting supporters. They lifted him on their shoulders, cheering as they carried him off. Meanwhile, the guards took Jeshua and dragged him to the cell that once held Barabbas.

Satisfied that justice had been served, the crowd dispersed. James and John came to Mary's aid. They carried her to the side of the square near a tree and administered to her head wound with cool water until she woke. They told her of the crowd's demand for Barabbas. She broke into tears.

"Mary, it is a terrible thing," James said. "But we have reason to believe that Pilate is friendly to our cause. We have sent word to him to hear our petitions."

Mary listened through her tears. John put his arm around her to comfort her.

"James, we should get inside near the warmth of a fire. She trembles so," John said.

***

Two days later, the rabbi appeared before the tribunal in shackles. There were no real charges against him because there was no evidence, except witnesses on behalf of the Sanhedrin and the Roman Senate. The sentence was not difficult to predict. Crucifixion would be the manner of his execution. Rome wanted to send a strong message to anyone who tried to influence the downfall of the Roman Empire by force, or undermine the people's faith.

Members of the Sanhedrin, as well as senatorial representatives from Rome, sat in on the sentencing. As Procurator of Judea, Pilate had the task of reading the rabbi's sentence.

"Jeshua Ben Joseph, rabbi and prophet, the so-called King of the Jews, you have been charged with sedition and blasphemy. It is the order of this tribunal that the punishment is death by crucifixion. You will be taken to the Great Temple where a tree will be shackled to you. You will drag the tree through the streets of Jerusalem for all to see. Your shame shall be public and you will be left to die on it. The designated place is also for all to see."

Jeshua looked at the members of the court and smiled. He dropped his head until the guards took him away to his cell until word came that his punishment tree was ready.

Later that night, Mary the Magdalene accompanied by James and John, requested an audience with Pilate.

John spoke first. "We have come to petition the Procurator to seek clemency for our Master, Jeshua Ben Joseph."

"It is too late," said Pilate.

"You are the law from Rome. Surely there must be something you can do?" James pleaded.

"I am sorry, but there is nothing. It is out of my hands."

"They said you were his friend. Is this is how Romans treat their friends?"

John asked.

"I did not want this. He brought it upon himself. He has too many enemies in high places."

Mary stepped forward. "Can you allow me to see him one more time?"

Pilate rapped nervously on his table. His frustration built and his rapping caused his wine cup to jump. He swept the cup from the table, sending it across the room.

"I warned him once and he did not even thank me. Why should I help you, or him?"

"I understand Jeshua better than anyone. He is a complex man and often preoccupied. He does not think of consequences, but he has a loving heart, a heart that I love dearly. All I ask is to see him before he dies. Can you extend your friendship one more time?"

Pilate stood up. "He is a foolish man to leave behind a woman who seems to love him as much as you. Guard, take this woman to detention cell number six. Give her as much time as she needs."

"By your command," the guard replied.

The guard descended three flights of steps to the lower detention level with Mary. He told the jailer to open the door to the holding cell area. The jailer took the heavy iron keys and unlocked the heavy wood and metal branded door. He struggled to push the door open, squeezing straw and mud aside.

The jailer entered with the guard and Mary followed behind. He asked, "Which one do you want?"

The guard turned to Mary. "Cell number six, please."

The jailer took the ring of keys to the cell at the end of the hall. He opened the door and exposed steps that led to the cell floor. She saw Jeshua chained to a set of rings mounted to a stone post. Straw was strewn on the floor, most of it piled waist deep into a corner.

Mary turned to the jailer. "Release him from the chains so we can be together."

The guard shrugged his shoulders. "What is the difference? He is not going anywhere."

The jailer laughed. "You are right. Call me when

you are ready to leave."

Mary descended the steps and sat nearby while he unlocked the shackles that kept Jeshua chained to the post.

"It smells down here," she said.

The jailer climbed the stairs toward the door. "This is not the palace, woman."

Once the jailer had left, Mary embraced Jeshua. He winced.

"What pains you?" she asked.

"My back. The wounds are still fresh."

She pulled back his robes to reveal the deep gashes that still oozed with drops of his blood. Tears streamed down her cheeks.

"How can God allow this to happen to you? I thought you were the chosen One?"

Jeshua said, "I am and I was, but the angel came and took the Father's witness from me. Now, my love, I am just a prophet given up for slaughter." He looked down. "I hoped that you would not see me like this. It is better that you remember me in another way."

"Jeshua, I do not care about that. We have only a short time left. Let us celebrate what little we have left in our last hour together."

They held each other and kissed. As they allowed their minds to join in a more pleasant place, Mary said, "Not all is lost my love. I am with child again."

Pilate's Gambit

I *could not sleep. The face of the Magdalene kept looming into view. Her words echoed inside my head. "Can you help us?" she said. I wrestled with myself. Had I done enough? I had given her time with the rabbi before his sentence. My mind was as quiet as a stone. Thoughts vanished while my mind listened to something I could not hear. There was a stirring inside my chest. A pressure near my heart arose. I thought perhaps an old wound had awakened. I told myself, "You are a fool. Don't be like an old woman." However, it was more than frustration, more than helplessness, and more than foolishness.*

Memories long forgotten crept in like shadows behind the falling sunset of my mind. A child's love strangled by the loss of a nonexistent family. A mother's love estranged by death at my birth and my father taken in battle before I could say his name. I believed the gods left me without brothers or sisters to make me strong. Now I realize it has also made me bitter.

It was too maddening to grasp. I struggled to trust the rabbi, yet not enough to embrace him. I argued with myself that I hardly knew him, and yet somehow I have always known him. I began to understand as the pain subsided. He showed me a way beyond my bitterness, beyond myself. I knew in my heart that this man must not die on the tree. His love must endure. I must save him and perhaps myself.

He will be crucified in a few days. How can I avoid this fact? To die on a tree usually takes days. It is customary to break their legs so the days become hours. Romans are not barbarians. We are civilized and have some sense of decency even with our manner of capital punishment. If the rabbi was a Roman citizen, we could make his death swift by the sword. The head is removed and that is that. What if we could avoid killing him, but make it look like we did? We could remove him safely from Rome's view, even from King Herod's view.

***

In the middle of the night, Pilate needed to speak with High Priest Caiaphas. The Procurator had an idea to change the rabbi's fate. What he had in mind would need the cooperation of others who felt as he did. Pilate believed himself to be a good judge of character, and in this moment, he had to trust his instincts about certain people. He counted on the true inner feelings of the high priest, and the fact that Caiaphas was also a politician.

In Pilate's experience, what politicians seemed to be on the surface was not always what lay underneath. If his plan was to work, he needed Caiaphas' help.

He went the Temple and requested a meeting. The attending priest was reluctant to awaken Caiaphas at the late hour, but Pilate was insistent and told him the matter was urgent. Caiaphas was very grumpy and entered the outer chamber full of complaints. He was not dressed in his priestly garb, only his night robes.

"This had better be important, Procurator. A priest cannot carry out the important tasks of God each day without proper rest."

"I apologize for waking you but I am troubled by the fate of the rabbi," said Pilate.

"We are all troubled in this matter, yet he walked a treacherous path that only could have ended in this manner."

"I beg to differ. I have a plan that might change the course. It is true that his sentence has been struck and must be carried out as the law demands. However, things that appear one way could actually be another."

Caiaphas stroked his beard cautiously, "I'm listening, Roman. What is brewing in that devious mind?"

"What if we could make it appear that the rabbi

dies on the tree but does not. If he is removed from public view, he can secretly make his escape from this debacle without anyone being the wiser."

"Just how might you accomplish this?"

"We end a condemned man's suffering by breaking his legs after several hours on the tree. This causes him to suffocate and die more quickly. There is nothing to say that we have to break the rabbi's legs."

"How does this apply to saving him? He is still crucified and you leave him to die within days. This is your solution?"

"You don't understand. This allows us the opportunity to offer the appearance of a timely death without carrying it out."

Caiaphas was not sure what Pilate was getting at but he had his attention. Pilate knew that his instincts about Caiaphas were correct. He had an ally, and the trick was to get him to agree. Pilate did not know how to fake the prophet's death, only to create the opportunity for it to unfold. He hoped that Caiaphas had something to offer. Priests have their own secrets and sometimes make good use of them when it serves their interests.

Caiaphas considered Pilate and his proposal. He realized what Pilate wanted. *The priesthood's true power lay in the bounty of secrets that bind them to nature's lesser-known truths,* thought Caiaphas, *and revealed only to the inner initiates of the order. Was saving the rabbi worth risking the revelation of such truths, and not even to a Jew but to a Gentile?*

"You ask too much of me, Roman. This is nothing short of sacrilege on my part," warned Caiaphas.

"I ask for no less than what I am willing to risk. What do you think will happen if this plan were revealed to my superiors and the Emperor? You would see my head roll down the street past the steps of the Great Temple, where you might only suffer the scorn of your brethren. Do you not regard him as I do? How often does such a man happen in this life? Is he not worth risking our own?" Pilate challenged.

"Your arguments are persuasive. You should have been a priest if not for your misfortune of not being born a Jew. That is not your fault. What I have to say must never be repeated. It is one of our most guarded of secrets."

Pilate smiled. "I give you my word, first as a Roman and second as a general."

Caiaphas sat down on a stone bench. He motioned for Pilate to sit near so that he could speak and no one hear what he was about to reveal.

"There is a sect of Jews near the Sea of Galilee not far from the abbey of Mount Carmel in a place called Nazareth. They are a stubborn group and adhere to the ancient ways. They are called the Essene

Brotherhood, an extremist group of ascetics that we frown on but tolerate."

"I have heard of them. Is not the rabbi also a Nazarene? Are not the Nazarenes members of this tribe?" asked Pilate.

"I am not sure that the rabbi follows them but I am told his father Joseph and mother Mary lived among these people. They practice an esoteric prayer by inducing a trance-like state. This crude method is an attempt to commune with God. We have discarded this method of devotion, which does not reflect the new and more enlightened Temple. They use a drug, an elixir that goes back to our tribe's roots in Sumeria and Babylonia. The drug induces a death-like state. It will perhaps suit your purpose."

"How can I obtain this drug and learn its use? I am Roman. I am sure they would not allow me to have it, let alone use it" said Pilate.

"I have already violated my vows of secrecy telling you of the drug. Contact the Essenes through the rabbi's followers. Some of them are of this sect and they may be willing to help you. I have done all I can. Now let me return to rest."

Pilate thanked Caiaphas for sharing his secret knowledge. Now he had the method but he was still at odds on how to make it happen. Time was short and he needed his wits to manage this clandestine scheme.

He returned to his chambers with a new problem.

"Octavius, come here," commanded Pilate. "The one they call James. Bring him to me at once."

Octavius was bewildered. "Where do I find this man? Is he not a follower of the rabbi? They are not wandering about the streets. Since we have captured their leader, they are hiding from us. I would bet my months wages they are buried beneath the city in the catacombs. They have every reason to believe we seek to crucify them all."

"Yes, but you must try. I have every confidence in you. They know that I am a friend to them more or less. James must be nearby because he attended to the rabbi's woman, the Magdalene. She is with the rabbi as we speak. Make it known that you seek James. Tell him that Pilate can help their cause. Let him know that I want to speak with him immediately."

"By your command," Octavius said. He smacked his breastplate and stormed from the chamber.

***

Octavius searched beyond the palace since the Magdalene woman was inside the dungeon with the rabbi. He did not have to go far. Men sat in the shadow of a small hovel and one looked familiar.

"You there," he said. "I am looking for James, a

follower of the rabbi."

The men got up and backed away for an escape.

Octavius spoke quickly to stop their retreat. "Do not run. I mean you no harm. The Procurator has news for James. He wants to help."

"Romans have made it clear that our lives are of no consequence and that we are to be hunted down like dogs and eliminated on the tree," declared John.

"I tell the truth. The Procurator must speak with the one called James immediately. He wants to help the rabbi."

"How is this possible? He sentenced our Master to death," said John.

"Pilate tried to grant him clemency and the crowds chose Barabbas. I beg of you, tell James that Pilate wants to see him."

John continued his argument until James held his hand against John's chest to stop him. He stepped forward.

"I am called James. What is so urgent that the Procurator talks of helping us when he refused before?"

"I am ordered to fetch you to the palace. He demanded that I find you as quickly as I could. Please come with me. No one else need know."

James turned to John and Andrew.

"It will be all right. Stay here and keep watch for

my return, but stay out of plain sight," James warned.

Octavius returned with James to the palace. He entered Pilate's chambers and reported, "I found him. Just as you predicted, he was close at hand."

"Thank the gods," said Pilate. "Welcome, James. This is very good that you have come. You are one of his closest. You were here before. I remember you now."

"Your soldier said that you are willing to help. What has changed your mind, Procurator?" James inquired.

Pilate poured wine for James and asked him to sit, and then began to speak.

"I don't know much about what I am about to say, but I'm sure the High Priest Caiaphas would not mind that I share this with you. He told me of a sect of Jews called the Essenes that live near Nazareth. He spoke of a ritual or spiritual practice that puts you into a deep sleep. I am not sure. But they use a special drug or elixir to accomplish this."

"Caiaphas told you of this?" James said. "I don't understand. I am a Nazarene and what you speak of is a secret of secrets among my people. I cannot believe he would tell a Roman such a thing. Yet you speak freely of it."

"He did tell me after much persuasion. You see, we both want to help the rabbi. I have a bold plan that will only work if I can obtain the elixir." Pilate said.

James leaned on a chair as he reeled from the revelation and request. He had questions that Pilate could not answer. James sat down trembling and began to accept the absurdity before him.

"Even if I could get the drug, why would you want it?" James asked.

"James, I have only this evening realized that the prophet man, Jeshua as you know him, is most important and his life must be preserved. I have a way in which that might be possible. If I tell you, you must swear by your God not to reveal it to anyone but the rabbi. Can you?"

James looked at him as though he were speaking another language. His mouth hung open and his mind seemed to loosen from its roots. "Procurator Pilate, I think perhaps our Father in heaven works through you. This is the only possible explanation. I am not supposed to swear, but if it means whether my Master lives or dies, then I shall make an exception. I, James of Alphaeus, do so foreswear."

Pilate explained his plan to James. With every word, James shook his head as if that could help him digest what Pilate was saying. Jeshua would be shackled to his tree as scheduled and carry the tree to a certain point in the city. Someone had to carry the tree for him while he was given the drug. He would fall asleep as though he has died, and then be removed to a safe place where he could be revived.

James interrupted. "You do not understand. The drug comes in two parts. The first is taken and then hours later, vinegar needs to be added before the person can go into a deep sleep. There is another problem. The drug can last as much as three days."

Pilate paused. "That is better still. We give him the drug and take him to the tree. When he asks for water, he will be given the vinegar instead. The rest can be dealt with as before."

"It might work but Golgotha is in plain view for those who want to watch the spectacle. How will you make this happen?"

"Perhaps we do not have to crucify him at Golgotha. Another suitable place can be used where we have control of the public. I will speak to Caiaphas about this."

"What will you do with him for three days?"

"I have not considered this," confessed Pilate.

"Only centurions are allowed to take a condemned man from a tree. Will that not risk your plan to exposure?"

"Yes. I thought of these ideas only hours ago. It is not one of my best strategies but I continue to try."

"Pilate, must he be crucified?"

"Without the crucifixion, the original problem

returns. He will be hunted and killed. Jeshua must be crucified, but he does not have to die on the tree. Can you have the drug within the next two days?"

"It will not be easy, although not impossible. I will leave for Nazareth at once."

Pilate was visibly relieved. He put his hand on James' shoulder and told him not to pass word to Mary of their meeting.

"The less she knows, the better. The Magdalene woman is a strong risk," said Pilate.

James agreed. He grabbed Pilate's shoulders and embraced him. "Bless you my brother. Be in peace."

Pilate waited for Mary to finish her visit with the rabbi. When she exited the palace, John was outside the gate to take her back to the inn.

***

Pilate went to cell number six and told Jeshua of his plan. The rabbi was reluctant.

"I am not sure of this action. I have seen my fate. It was shown to me by the angel Melchizedek in the garden before I was taken, and it is my Father's Will that this be so."

Pilate could not digest the angel story, but accepted it for the moment. "How do you know that your God has not planned this from the beginning, and uses me as a tool to accomplish his Will?"

Jeshua was silent.

"I ask again," said Pilate. "How do you know that your God has not planned this?"

The rabbi did not want to die and he yielded to Pilate, with the condition that Mary was told of the plan. Pilate said that her life would be in danger if she knew what was going to happen. Jeshua reluctantly agreed.

"Will you see to it that she is moved to a safer place like Gaul when this is over? She is with child."

Pilate promised that he would.

The View of Golgotha

Two soldiers on horseback preceded the log of olive wood as it was dragged over the stones of the street. The horse hooves clopping together with the log bobbing on the stones made for a strange rhythm.

The crucifixion tree was hewn and had its bark removed especially for the rabbi. The centurions stopped at the Great Temple for him. They released the harness that held the tree, and it fell to the street with a solid tone that rang out as it slapped the stones. When the rabbi arrived, they attached his shackles to the tree so that he could haul it by himself.

We Romans are an efficient people. Trees are prized commodities and nothing is wasted on men condemned to death. Most crucifixion trees are used many times, but a new tree was made for the rabbi. It was a single pole with a small step added half way down as a rest for his feet.

They had carved a placard from a small piece of chittum wood with the inscription, Yod-Nun-Resh-Yod, and filled in the letters with his blood. It meant "Jesus of Nazareth King of the Jews." The day was warm by *mid morning and humidity hung in the air. The sun was bright but sheltered behind a hazy cloud.*

I knew what I had to do, but I took no joy in it. Even though my plan was unfolding as I wished, it left me no pleasure knowing what the rabbi was to endure. Sometimes by necessity, I have attended the crucifixion of murderers, thieves, and insurrectionists. By Roman law, I am supposed to witness this man's crucifixion, too, but my heart is heavy. I cannot watch his suffering. I already have visions of his torture resting uncomfortably in the back of my mind.

I stood there and watched while they attached his chains and shackles to the tree. He struggled to lift it but the log was too heavy. I never thought about the heaviness until now. Strange that we administer hard labor before we hang the condemned. Perhaps we are not as civilized as I thought.

The rabbi looked at me after the guard on foot administered the whip against him. He closed his eyes from the pain but did not cry out. Then the guard yelled, " move along you slime."

My jaw clenched as the whip landed on older marks. I watched him drag that tree until he turned the corner to the adjoining street. The walk to Golgotha would be a long and agonizing if he were going that far. Fortunately, he would not have so very long to go. His size and weight did not match the task before him.

The prophet man was weak and thin. His wounds bled from his whipping. They would have left the crown of thorns on his head but I ordered them to remove it.

I explained to the guards that walked with him that if he fell, they were to obtain someone else to carry the tree for him. They were to take him to a side street and wait for a physician to give him medicine so he might be strong enough to endure the pain he would experience on the tree. I knew they would understand that. They accepted my instructions and did not question me.

There were many from the city that watched. Some of the women wept to see him in such a state. Others were less sympathetic. They called him names, threw garbage, and spit on him. Others threw rocks, while the guards tried to protect him. It was not that they cared. They were responsible to get him to the crucifixion alive.

The rabbi fell earlier than I expected. He was too far from the meeting place for a replacement, and he was whipped until he got back to his feet and continued toward the rendezvous point. As he walked the trail, he did so with bare feet. Roman law forbade the condemned to wear any foot coverings. By the time the rabbi reached the rendezvous, the torn flesh and blood of his feet matched the rest of his body.

***

Jeshua fell a second time only two streets from the rendezvous. Unshackled from the tree, the guards dragged him to an alley and searched for an able-bodied man to replace him. Simon of Cyrene was on his way to complete business in Jerusalem and stopped at the sight of Jeshua lying on the street. The guards hailed him.

"This criminal can no longer carry the tree. You will carry it for him," they said.

Simon hefted the log and could not lift it beyond his chest. He tried twice without success. The guards lifted the tree for him and placed the heavy log on his back. Simon steadied his footing before he moved forward.

Meanwhile, a guard hoisted Jeshua with his arm over the guard's shoulder while another guard helped with his arm around the rabbi's waist. The three hobbled down the alley where they were to meet the physician. They did not have to wait because James, John, and Andrew and Gideon, an Essene from Nazareth, were ready for them.

Gideon administered the first part of the elixir to Jeshua from a small goatskin bag that he took from his sling. The taste was bitter. James wiped his mouth after three sips of the drug.

"That should be enough," said James.

Gideon withdrew the goatskin and said to the guards, "Give him a few moments. His strength will return and he will be able to walk again."

Guards at Golgotha had dug a deep enough hole for the tree to set into the ground so that it would not fall with the wind. The tree waited for its captive. It was almost mid-day when the group arrived. John, James, and Andrew split off with Gideon and stood aside while the guards laid Jeshua on his back. They wasted no time in preparing his body for the nailing. The first guard brought a large wooden maul and two iron spikes from his leather bag. The second guard took Jeshua's hands and brought his arms over his head with his hands crossed, one over the other. He held them there while the first guard placed the long spike over his wrists. He raised the maul over his head and brought it down hard on the spike. The spike entered Jeshua's flesh easily but resisted further penetration because of the bones.

Jeshua did not cry out from the first blow. With another powerful strike, the spike split the wrist bones with an awful cracking. Jeshua screamed, and nature reacted as well. The wind blew in strong gusts as though a great tempest was about to burst. Just as the first guard had finished with Jeshua's wrists and prepared his feet with a heavy blow to the insteps crossed one over the other, a thunderclap rocked the countryside like an earthquake had struck. Jeshua cried out again as his foot bones spread to allow the hard metal to pass into the olive wood beneath. The guards pulled on his arms and legs to confirm that the body of the rabbi was firmly attached. Other Roman soldiers gathered to lift the tree into the hole. Jeshua did not make a sound.

Clouds darkened the sky above. Thunder roared over the countryside and lightning reached from one cloud to another, like a disapproval from heaven. Onlookers cowered and looked for hiding places from the lightning. The sun darkened, casting a strange dull light. Fear poured into everyone's heart and all knew that something about this event was not right in heaven. The Romans feared that their gods were angry. The followers of Jeshua believed their God was angry, too.

**

More time passed. Jeshua raised his head and said, "Father, forgive them for they are ignorant of what they do."

Four centurions sat at the base of the tree casting dice, betting on how long the rabbi would live and who would win his crimson robe as a souvenir. They heard him cry in a weakened voice, "I have thirst...give me water. Please give me water."

A guard got up to take him an urn of water but was stopped. "Do not use this one. Give him a drink from the pail near the tree."

At the foot of the tree was the pail placed by Gideon. Inside was a sponge. The guard smelled the liquid and realized that it was vinegar. He laughed at this along with the others.

"The king is thirsty," he said. "We cannot let him suffer."

The guard leaned a ladder against the tree. He stabbed his sword into the sponge soaked with vinegar. He climbed to Jeshua and extended the sponge to his mouth. Jeshua sucked at the sponge. He looked to the sky and said, "Unto my Father, I commend my spirit."

Lightning struck in three places around the tree. Everyone fled. Thunderclaps continued while Jeshua's body fell limp upon the tree. He did not move anymore. The onlookers and guards watched in awe. One guard ran away and screamed, "We have killed the Messiah! We are doomed!"

Dark clouds poured rain as people emerged from their hiding places and dispersed. The spectacle was over. The devoted followers that remained had stayed and allowed to collect the Master from the tree. Mary sat weeping before the tree, soaked to the skin. As directed, the guards left them alone. James and Andrew removed and received him into a white linen cloth while John went to Mary and comforted her. The body was wrapped like swaddling cloth and carried on their shoulders.

Joseph of Arimathea had a family tomb not far from the crucifixion site. The tomb was a cave roughly cut into a hillside. His followers carried the rabbi inside and placed him on a slab of stone.

Mary, Martha, and Sarah lifted the linen cloth to reveal Jeshua. Mary said, "So many wounds, so much pain. I wish I could have suffered for him."

She placed her hand on his chest and looked at his face. He looks like he is sleeping, she thought, his face is so peaceful. She wept and the others held her until they were able to set their feelings aside and focused on the task. The women opened their bags and laid out the anointing oils they had brought for him.

They rubbed his body with the oils while Mary tenderly massaged his temples with myrrh and frankincense. She murmured prayers for his swift delivery to the realm of the Father God. Every touch said goodbye. With every tear, she extended her heart and wished that she could be with him. At the same time she felt her womb active with her child and suffered the sorrow and loss that he would not know his children. She was also grateful for his offspring.

Soon the task was completed and all departed except Mary. She stayed to share with Jeshua what she had not said to him before. She apologized for the harshness she expressed on many occasions, the disdain and challenge to him that came from her judgment. Mary expressed her secret admiration and jealousy of his connection to the Father, and her competition with him to rule the other disciples.

She promised to do her best to help the disciples and guide them. They were weak and needed the strength of her spirit. Finally, she thanked him for the wisdom he gave her, his trust and devotion, and most of all for the constant love and support he had shown. As she left the tomb, she looked back and wondered if God would allow them to come together again at a future time. It was then she knew how much she would miss his tender caress and love.

Mary's Vision

I had gone to the Great Temple and met with Caiaphas after James left for Nazareth. There, Nicodemus and Joseph of Arimathea joined us to go over my plan once more. I explained the issues brought up by James, along with my concerns.

Joseph was most eager to help. He offered the use of his land and family tomb. Joseph was honored to have the crucifixion there. Those who wanted to watch the rabbi crucified could do so from some distance. The mound of Golgotha was in plain view. More than this, Joseph knew the old practices of using the drug and offered his tomb to lay Jeshua until he revived. It was a perfect ruse for the public to witness the burial of the rabbi. I was grateful that the rabbi had other true friends to support him.

The situation in Rome has grown more complicated. Emperor Tiberius left for Capri because he was weary of the political intrigue in Rome. In truth, he wanted to carry on his debaucheries away from prying eyes under the guise of semi-retirement. Sejanus was named Regent in his stead. Sejanus in turn, had appointed several important positions in his absence. One of those was mine.

Sejanus also eliminated any of Tiberius' competition for the throne in his absence. On the surface, this seemed to be a loyal action on behalf of the Emperor, but in truth, his ambition included the throne for himself. His goal was to eliminate Tiberius in Capri as his final act, prior to ascending to the throne.

Part of Sejanus' plot was to integrate his power through the Julians by involving himself with Lavilla, Tiberius' niece. He wanted to become an adoptive Julian by marriage, and gain the support of the Julians not supportive of Tiberius. Thus, he could consolidate his base of power and ascend to the throne unquestioned as next in line. Lavilla turned out to be a problem for him, and he withdrew from her. As a scorned woman, she informed Tiberius of Sejanus' plans before she could be implicated. Unfortunately for Sejanus, in response to this news, Tiberius wrote a letter to the Senate accusing Sejanus of treachery and treason, and had him executed along with the Julians that supported him.

My position in Judea is now in question. I fear that having the rabbi appear to be executed is not enough to resolve questions of my loyalty to the Emperor. I am also at odds with my promise to the rabbi to make sure his wife, Mary the Magdalene, will leave for Gaul with some measure of safety.

Since the rabbi was crucified, the rest of his followers have made themselves scarce. James and John, as well as the fisherman called Peter, do not repeat his words openly. They do not even speak of the rabbi as a friend. On the night of his capture, Peter more than once denied knowing him. They ran from the garden to save their own skins. These so-called followers are a miserable lot of spineless cowards. I would trust any centurion with my life in their stead.

What am I to do with the Magdalene? Prudence suggests I should wait until this matter settles before I attempt to move her. My plan is not yet complete. I must get the rabbi out of the tomb and away from Jerusalem. I hear that his woman believes that he can rise from the dead. I am bound to keep silent.

***

In the middle of the night, Mary woke exceptionally hot. The room was quiet and peaceful. She was about to go back to sleep when a light appeared. She felt a prickling sensation as the light became brighter. Mary watched in fright. The light coalesced into a form that appeared to be a man. This changed and spread into what seemed like a large bird. When the form finished, the creature was both

Mary's Vision

man and bird.

It spoke to her. "Mary... Do not be afraid. I am Melchizedek, an angel come to reveal the truth about Jeshua. In three days, he will rise. His tribulation is over and the Father is pleased. It is important that you tell the others, for some have lost their joy and passion because of his tribulation. Be aware that he cannot be with you any longer. It is important that you go to the place called Gaul as soon as you can. It will no longer be safe for you here. However, rejoice, for a new world is upon you and you shall inherit it."

"Will I be with him in heaven?" she said with tears falling.

"There is an eternity waiting for you. In the eyes of the Father, you are already one. Blessed be the Father and his Kingdom."

The angel dissolved within the receding light until the room was dark again. Mary awoke and found she was soaked. She burned with fever. Mary called out to John but he did not answer. She slept until morning. This time when she called out to John, he came to her door.

"You talked in your sleep. Are you well?" he asked.

"I am fine but in the middle of the night I was very hot and could not sleep. A strange dream woke me," Mary reported. "An angel appeared and told me about Jeshua. I would never see him again. He said he had arisen and would be with me in heaven."

John was startled by this news. "The dream falls on the heels of your loss. We shall all miss him."

Mary bowed her head. She looked at John with tears. "I grew up with my father. He taught me many things, most of all to be strong and independent. I learned what I could about his business and was very useful to him. I had hoped that it would be the same for Jeshua. Now he is gone and I have nothing but sorrow. I gladly yielded my independence for his sake, and because I loved him."

"I understand how you feel. Actually, we all gave up our independence for his sake because we too loved him. Many in the group are angry with you, since the beginning. It was not easy for us to work closely with a woman, and very difficult to be cared for by a woman. I watched the Master become even greater after you joined us. For that I am grateful. I have grown to appreciate what you have done for us. It is why I asked to travel with you and protect you. I believe you are in more danger now than before. The Master has many enemies and they seek to stamp out those who were left behind. You must leave this place soon before matters get worse."

"The angel in my dream said that I should go to Gaul," said Mary.

"The others are frightened for their lives and hide

in the shadows. Little is said about doing the work the Master wanted. Peter has tried several times to speak to the elders in the synagogue, but they scorn him as they did the Master. Peter is lost in his lamenting. He only talks about how bad things are since the Master passed."

Mary put on her outer robes. John looked on inquisitively. "Where are you going?" he asked.

"My husband's body needs attending. I shall go to the tomb and tend to him."

"The tomb has been sealed with a large stone. You cannot move it without considerable help. Even I am not enough to help."

"Then I will ask the Romans. It's the least they can do," she said defiantly.

"Mary, you are being stubborn again and that will not help."

"If you know me well, once I set my mind to do something, nothing gets in my way."

"Far be it from me to get in your way," said John.

Mary set out for the tomb where Jeshua had been placed. She finally arrived at the foothills and mounted the last steps allowing her to see the tomb's entrance. She was outraged that the stone had been moved. Her eyes welled with tears as she rushed to the entrance that no one was left to guard.

Inside she found only an empty stone slab and the

linen draped back as though a sleeper had turned back the bedding to arise. The body of Jeshua was gone. She fell to the stone floor. Why would anyone steal her husband's body? Then she remembered what the angel had said.

She caressed the linen cloth that had been laid over his body. Her heart ached. She lamented that she did not have his body to touch anymore. Her emotions kept shifting. She wondered about the dream and whether it was real. Other questions began to roll around in her mind. Why were no Roman soldiers left to guard the tomb? If they stole his body, where would they take it?

Mary knew that she was trying to rationalize the obvious truth. He had arisen from the dead as he said he would. She needed to tell the others right away.

***

Mid-morning of the third day after the crucifixion, Mary went to the bazaar outside the city and left a message for the disciples. She told them to meet her in the catacombs later that night. At nightfall, she went to the designated rendezvous and all were present. They chastised her for calling the meeting because it was far too risky to reveal their hiding place.

Thomas attacked first. "Mary, you do not have the

Mary's Vision

authority to call a meeting here. Only Peter can."

"I was under the impression that any disciple can call us together if it was urgent. What I have to say is urgent enough," she snapped back.

Simon the Zealot spoke next. "We are here at the risk of our lives. It had better be urgent."

"Mary, they are right," said Peter. "You have no right to call us. Only James or myself that can do such a thing, not a ..."

"A woman! Mary interrupted.

"You can have your silly rules. I really do not care. But I have earned the right because I bought and paid for your lives these last three years. This is the thanks I get? I do not know why I bother to bring you this news. God knows you do not deserve this."

"Do not add blasphemy to your other indiscretions," chastised Peter.

"Is this what the Master wanted from all of you? Did he really want you to spend the rest of your days hiding in the shadows? You are all pathetic!" Mary retorted.

"Mary, please ignore them," said James. "They are frightened and feel their loss, as you do. Tell us, what news?"

"Jeshua has arisen!" she exclaimed.

"What do you mean?" Peter asked.

"The Master has arisen from the dead. I went to

tend to his body and found the stone turned away. Inside, only the linen cloth remained. He has arisen I tell you."

John and Thomas tried to speak at once, until John yielded to Thomas. "I don't believe you. I saw the Romans stick their spears into his side and his blood run free. I watched as he gave up his spirit on the tree to the Father God. It is not right, Mary, what you are doing. We are grieving for him and you rub our noses in his death. Now you want us to believe that he defeated his own death? How do you know the Romans have not rolled away the stone and stolen his body?"

"Thomas, how can you speak like this after all I have done? You have lost a teacher, but I have lost a teacher and a husband."

"I vote that we go to the tomb and examine it for ourselves, to confirm what Mary has revealed," said James. "If the Romans stole the body, there will be signs of desecration."

John agreed and the rest came around to agree with James as well. James added, "I believe we are jealous of Mary again. She has seen to his care even after his death. We have not even visited his grave to give our respects. It is high time that we did."

Only James knew about the plan to save Jeshua. He was not accustomed to lying to his closest friends but keeping the secret from the rest insured the most important goal, to keep Jeshua alive. He especially hated lying to Mary. Her report of Jeshua's ascension might become more important than his survival. His death and resurrection could be a symbol for all of his teachings, and a demonstration to all future believers. Her story exemplified Jeshua's words about the importance of the inner spiritual life and the ultimate survival of life beyond death.

***

Jeshua had been safely transported to Egypt, and stayed among the Egyptian priests. They were aware of his importance to the world. Jeshua could continue his work and no one would know the truth. The Egyptian priesthood had as many secrets as the Essene. They opened the left paw of the great Sphinx and brought Jeshua to the ancient caverns and rivers below used by the followers of Isis. Pilate was assured that the rabbi would be safe to continue his important spiritual work. A special connecting tunnel in the Great Pyramid led to the king's chamber and allowed him to travel anywhere on earth or to the stars, as the priests and pharaohs had done centuries before.

The details were far too mysterious for Pilate. He took them at their word that the rabbi would be out of harm's way.

Pilate went to the bazaar where Octavius had found James. He spoke to a Muslim dealer named Akhmed about James. Akhmed claimed he knew no one by that name, or any of the prophet's followers. With a few well-placed drachmas across his palm, he changed his mind. Pilate informed the dealer that it was a matter of life and death for the Magdalene woman and he became more cooperative.

Akhmed said that they had one who would come to check for any news from their other friends. He told Pilate to leave a message and he would pass it along. Pilate was reticent but realized he had no choice but to trust the man. He said he was looking for James and that it was urgent he come to the palace as soon as possible. The dealer took his money. He bit into the coins, and assured him he would pass along the message.

Pilate did not trust the dealer any more than he would trust a whore to leave his money after she serviced him. Nevertheless, he had no choice in the matter. He had to wait until James came to him.

Almost a day went by before a young boy appeared at the palace gates demanding to see Pilate. Pilate heard the argument between the boy and the guards and intervened.

"What do you want, boy? Are you hungry? I am

feeling generous today. Have a meal, compliments of your Procurator," Pilate said, as he threw coins to what he thought was a simple beggar.

Pilate turned to go back inside, but the boy spoke as he picked up the coins. "I have come to give you a message from James."

"What did you say?"

"I have a message. James asked that you meet him at the bazaar just after dark."

"Tell him it is done. Do you have family, boy?" Pilate inquired.

"Yes, Procurator," he said.

"Feed them as well," said Pilate, and threw more coins.

"Thank you. You are most kind."

"Sometimes I am, on the good days."

The boy disappeared into the late afternoon crowd. Pilate stopped by the Great Temple and asked for Joseph of Arimathea. After a few moments, Joseph appeared at the doors. He greeted Pilate with the usual courtesy. Pilate told Joseph how much he appreciated his generosity toward the rabbi.

Joseph waved his hand. "It was nothing. I wanted to do more for my teacher. At least I helped ensure that he could go on spreading the word."

Pilate told Joseph of his promise to Jeshua for Mary's safe passage to Gaul, along with anyone who wished to join her. Joseph was puzzled.

"Why ask me? Surely you could escort her with soldiers sufficient for her safety."

"Even now there are those who would seek to destroy any remnant of the rabbi. It would be good that she at least had the sanction of the Temple. Will you do that for Jeshua?" Pilate asked.

Joseph thought for a moment. "I must have release from the High Priest Caiaphas to travel far but I will seek it immediately."

Soon it was dark and time for Pilate's rendezvous with James. When he arrived at the bazaar, James waited for him. They went inside an inn to a small table near the back and out of view of passersby, and ordered wine.

"What is so urgent, Procurator?" James asked.

"I like a man who is direct. You are such a man, James. I have arranged for the Magdalene to leave tonight for Gaul. I want you to travel with her and anyone who wants refuge away from Jerusalem. Joseph will travel with you to provide legitimate reasons to be on Temple business. If you stay much longer here, I believe you will follow your Master's fate on one of Rome's trees."

"Very well. I shall ask John to join us, and return after I tell Mary of our escape. We are in your debt, Pilate. Peace be with you."

Paul's Challenge

After a year had passed since the rabbi's exile to Egypt, few in Jerusalem spoke of him anymore, if at all. People in different villages in Judea did report seeing him from time to time. I assumed this was a form of hysteria or sickness. The oddity of those reports was that they spread to such diverse places simultaneously. I believed they came from people's inability to cope with the loss.

Paul informed me in a letter that he was going to Asia in hopes of encouraging Gentiles to hear his version of Jeshua's words. Frankly, this disturbed me. It seemed that he had shifted in his direction and intention. Paul was adamant about undermining the rabbi for Rome's sake, yet he wanted to carry the rabbi's words to other cultures. His action was in direct opposition to Rome.

I wrote him a reply that told of my concerns about the purpose of his journey. I asked if he had become a convert to the rabbi's teachings, and told how risky the venture would be. His answer said that he had not become a convert but saw an opportunity to express insights he developed while traveling with the rabbi. He had many ideas of his own that differed from the rabbi, and that his ideas were equally important, if not greater. He perceived his new role was to organize and unify the Christian movement, not under the guise of what the rabbi taught, but to rally the would-be followers to take another path. This would serve to ultimately undermine the rabbi's approach. His purpose was to realign those who followed the rabbi and redirect their thinking to be more compatible with Roman interests.

I wrote another letter to ask how his ideas differ from those of the rabbi. Paul replied quickly and at length. He was already on board a ship bound for the East and used the time to write.

Paul defined a fundamental difference with those who represented the movement in Jerusalem. Before he left, he argued with James and Peter, the fisherman. Their view fixed around the central theme that a true follower must adhere to the strict principle of eliminating the unclean foreskin of the male genitals by circumcision. In addition, they disagreed over the adoption of strict dietary laws as set down by Moses.

The rabbi often said that the way was for all men, Jew and Gentile alike, argued Paul. In his opinion, the rabbi suggested that they put aside the old practice regarding the uncleanliness of the body. They were not important and instead were to be seen as metaphorical. He believed this was a symbol for the uncleanliness of the spirit. Cut away the unclean parts of the spirit that might corrupt a man's life, and rely on faith in the rabbi's way. Unlike the Jewish tradition, it becomes an oral tradition.

Paul could not persuade the elders of the Jerusalem synagogue to accept the insight, and they forbade him to teach his corruption of the rabbi's words in other lands. Paul said that the rabbi demanded his followers carry the teaching to all and they, unlike him, remained in hiding. He claimed to be the only one committed to the rabbi's request. Paul revealed that he did not leave the disciples in Jerusalem with a sanction of what he was doing.

He went on about the rabbi's woman, the Magdalene, and how she had created dissention among the disciples. Hardly anyone in the group approved of her but they would never challenge the rabbi out of respect for him. They generally disliked her. Paul intended to include his negative views about the involvement of women in religious activities and responsibilities in his treatises, and add the rabbi's sanction of his opinions. Though he expressed his judgment against the rabbi's liberal attitude toward women to me, what he wrote to others was the opposite.

***

Paul was gone for three years before I heard from him again. He returned to Jerusalem to attempt reconciliation with the synagogue. He found the other disciples destitute and starving. Drought had stricken the land and food was scarce. The negative opinions about the rabbi's teachings left the disciples as outcasts. Mary was secretly living in Gaul and without her financial support the disciples were left to fare for themselves. Paul was surprised at the contrast between the conditions in Jerusalem and the abundance in the lands he traveled. He tried to join the pockets of supporters in the East to the Great Temple in Jerusalem. Once again, the High Priest rejected his interpretation of the rabbi's teachings. Despite the rejection, he brought great wealth from the tithing offered by the other groups of followers, which Paul now called churches.

Saddened by the their reluctance to yield to his bid for the joining of Jerusalem and the Asia, he planned to return and continue to travel on to other parts of Europe. In one of his letters he said that a new follower called Barnabas expressed keen interest in his ideas. He wanted to support Paul's efforts.

Paul's Challenge

Barnabas even asked to join Paul on his return to the Asia, and work with him to build and expand his work. The task to maintain a close connection with all the little churches was sometimes more than Paul could bear. He fell ill on several occasions, leaving Barnabas to speak to the new people.

***

Peter was troubled about the lack of response to Paul's efforts in the synagogue in Jersualem. He believed they were ungrateful to Paul for reviving the work in Jerusalem with his financial support. After several months passed, he decided to go to Asia and see what Paul was doing. He could help Paul make his case to the synagogue through an impartial view on return from his mission.

He found Paul in Thessalonica. There, friendly Greeks greeted him with a banquet of many foods. He was reluctant to eat with them because of his dietary commitments as a Jew. Paul encouraged him to dine out of a sense of diplomatic and spiritual protocol. He recanted his dietary commitments and joined in the feast. Peter noticed the unusually friendly men around Paul. They behaved more like lovers than friends. Paul returned their favors as well. He drew Paul aside at the first chance and questioned him.

Paul admitted that the Greeks had unusual sexual appetites and believed it only fair that he share in their culture to convince them that the way of the rabbi could be adapted to their daily lives. Peter was shocked. It was wrong to indulge in debauchery that defiled the body and diminished the spirit. Paul disagreed. Peter realized that perhaps it was Paul's predilection. He had never known him to long for the loins of a woman. He had never married nor did he ever mention any desire for such union.

Peter's Second Betrayal

I learned about Peter's visit from one of Paul's letters. His sexual conduct with the Greeks was unacceptable among his Judean counterparts. Along with this, I suspected that his hostile attitude toward women contributed to his harsh rules of conduct regarding marriage and divorce.

One year later, near the end of my stay in Judea, I was saddened to hear from Gaius Levinius, a member of the Senate in Rome, that the Consul had raised charges against Paul. Unfortunately, all of the letters he sent to Asia were in question. His relationships with Christians of other nations were considered alliances with enemies of Rome. Therefore Caligula, the new consul, considered Paul seditious. He demanded his return to Rome for questioning. Paul gladly agreed, hoping to show his plan for a resolution with the Christian problem. Caligula believed Paul was the problem. He was tried and found guilty, and beheaded according to Roman Law.

More intrigue followed in Rome, with the Consul seat left for the one most clever. The rumor was that Caligula murdered Tiberius while he was sleeping in his semi-retirement quarters in Capri. With Sejanus out of the way, Caligula seemed the most likely culprit, because he was now able and free to ascend to the Consul seat without challenge.

The pressure on me from Tiberius was now removed. Before his demise on Capri, Tiberius had kept himself busy eliminating Sejanus' appointments. I did not realize that my behavior in Judea made for a negative record that indicated my inability to manage justice with a measure of prudence. My temper and impatience was no secret among my centurions, but no one complained because brutality seemed a normal feature of a Roman officer. However, there were many complaints from the Jews and Samaritans in Jerusalem.

My style of management was harsh but effective. That was not the real problem for Caligula. He meted out his own brand of cruelty in Rome, and as I have heard, extended that cruelty and perverse sexuality to members of his family. The real problem for Caligula was that some of my actions prompted an invasion from the Queen of the Aksum Empire. He summoned me to Rome to answer for my actions.

Meanwhile, he made Herod Agrippa the governor of Judea. My position as Procurator remained for the moment but Caligula significantly reduced my power to govern Judea.

I delayed my journey by explaining that there were many delicate local matters unique to my knowledge, and that someone without this knowledge would have great difficulty with the transition. I convinced Caligula of the importance of the delay by instilling fear in Herod Agrippa. I told him that beginning his governorship with incompetence in handling these matters would reflect negatively in Rome. Leaving Agrippa to mull over the possibility meant that I could count on an immediate communication from him to Caligula.

The time I needed was to create a retreat path, if necessary. All good officers create a path of retreat. Having the courage to face your enemy is one thing, but there is an old military adage that says if the odds are insurmountable and all avenues of engagement considered are unworkable, beat a quick retreat and live to fight another day.

Logic suggested that I had a good case for my defense but I could not be certain of how it would weigh with Caligula. Unlike Tiberius, Caligula is notorious for his lack of reason and irrational outbursts of anger. His arrogant style of rule could only make enemies quickly in the Senate, and that group is a hive of villainy one does not want to alienate.

His rapid rise to power as Consul and Emperor

surprised me. Tiberius' rule, though effective, left a bad taste in the mouths of those who longed for a return to the old Republic. The Senate's reluctance to give over to the whims of a dictator is evident from the assassination of Gaius Julius Caesar. It is always precarious for the Republic when instability and fear engender a desire for a charismatic and powerful individual to assume control, who suggests that absolute rule is more efficient against the existence of chaos than the inefficiency of a democratic Republic. It gives me heartache to witness such dark days in Rome. Watching her suffer at the hand of such incompetence is almost too much to bear.

Three months later, I could not sustain any further delay to return to Rome. On the other hand, I did look forward to her, as a child would feel after leaving home for the chance of a great adventure. During this time I had planned my escape, if necessary. When I arrived, the city seemed to be overwhelmed with agitation. Soldiers were busy arresting citizens everywhere I turned. I was somehow invisible and unimportant. Caligula waited two full days after my arrival before he summoned me to court. In the meantime, I had a chance to learn many things.

The most significant was that the fisherman Peter was also in Rome. I wanted to see him. Perhaps his fate intertwines with mine. As I approached the outer atrium of the Senate, praetorian guards joined me on either side, escorting me as we ascended the steps. At the top, I looked down to see priests releasing doves into the air as homage to Zeus. Several large marble pillars flanked the entrance, supporting a long marble and limestone impediment with archers riding chariots carved on both sides, depicting battles won by great warriors of the past.

The floor of the Senate was polished marble inlaid with geometric designs, and the room echoed with murmurs from senators flanked on three sides, sitting in togas on stone risers. Many members of the Senate represented the various classes of family aristocracy. Caligula was in the center and off to the side in the Consul's seat. Though the situation was solemn, I was in awe at the pomp of the formal proceedings. It was then that I realized how long I had been away from home.

I had expected to be the first on the docket, and was surprised to see Peter stand before Caligula, while I waited my turn for the Emperor's audience.

Once I was comfortable in these surroundings, my attention fell on the exchange between Peter and Caligula.

"Fisherman, what say you to my offer?" began Caligula.

"I do not understand what you want of me," replied

Peter.

"Your Emperor does not speak plainly enough for you? Perhaps the desert dust has filled your ears and you no longer hear us. If you want to save the lives of your brethren, give me the location of the rabbi's woman, the Magdalene. Do this and I will spare the lives of your precious friends. Is that plain enough for you?"

Peter did not respond. I wondered if he would succumb to the Emperor. He vacillated over the decision he was about to make and looked around the room until he caught my eye. For a moment we stared at each other and I saw his shame at betraying the Magdalene roll over his face like a dark cloud.

***

Peter bowed his head. "You will find her in the southern provinces of Gaul."

"That is more like it," the Emperor crowed. "I shall spare your friends as you wish. Now go away from my sight. You disgust me."

The fisherman left the room and the senators voiced a loud jumble of grumbling. Senacus Aurelius, a Julian, said, "Emperor, how can you agree to this bargain? The Christians will always be a source of great unrest. They stir the people against us every day."

Caligula stood and adjusted his toga. "Do you take your Emperor to be a fool, Senacus? Everyone in this august body knows how I feel about the Christians. I would execute them all but that would interfere with my plans. The Magdalene woman is our greatest threat. She was closest to the rabbi. She is the most loyal to him, even after his death. You need not worry about the fisherman and his pathetic friends. As you can see, he would also sell their skins if it suited him. They are of no concern to me. I will have them slaughtered soon enough."

The mood shifted as the senators became quiet and Caligula returned to his seat.

"Bring in the next case," he demanded.

A praetorian guard of the Senate announced, "We present Pontius Pilate, Procurator of Judea."

Pilate walked out to senators, some whose faces he recognized and many he did not. He nodded respectfully before bowing before the Emperor Caligula. He regarded Pilate with admiration and intended nonchalance. He arose from his seat to circle the Procurator as if to study an object he was about to buy in the marketplace.

"You stand before us accused of brutality and cruelty to the Samaritans and citizens of Judea," said Caligula. "Personally, I believe they should get everything they deserve. Some of your behavior in

Judea I can abide by, as I never liked the Jews. They smell and are far too self-serving.

"I am ready to dismiss those charges. However, your actions have brought an invasion from the Aksum Empire. This crime we cannot ignore. What say you?"

Pilate replied, "Emperor, I have always honored and served Rome and, as many know, I have fought and won many battles for her glory. I accepted the assignment as Procurator of Judea without reluctance. Given the lack of success of my predecessors, I have kept the peace by ruling an often rebellious and hostile people with an iron hand. I have even successfully caught, tried, and executed one of the most insidious rebels, the rabbi from Nazareth, the leader of the Christian movement.

"The incident involving the Queen of Aksum and her invasion was a simple matter of pride. I escorted her armies over the border, pursuant to a threat. She had to invade in order to save face with her armies. Her army was no match for the highly trained centurions at my disposal and she knew that. So I allowed the so-called invasion to occur only to appease her delicate political situation."

"The Queen sent a formal complaint to Rome," said Caligula. "That was an embarrassment for your Emperor. Given the details of your explanation, I shall forego your execution. You will be stripped of your rank and status as a Roman officer, forfeiting all entitlements of Roman lands and wealth, and hereby exiled. Now go before I have a change of heart."

Pilate bowed before the Emperor and thanked him for his leniency. From the court he went to the sunny precipice that led to the steps below. On the lower tier of steps Peter was arguing with a man from Phrygia called Simon Magus. Pilate approached and Peter turned to receive him.

"You are the one called Pontius Pilate, the Procurator that helped to save our Master," said Peter.

"Yes, that is correct," said Pilate. "I can say he was a friend. Can you say that as well? I was present in the courtroom as you betrayed the Magdalene. I cannot stomach a traitor and you are that. How can you claim to be his friend and be a party to his woman's death? If there be a punishment for you I wish it could be a hundred fold what your Master suffered for you."

"You do not understand. Mary was his woman, but also arrogant and carried herself like she was better than the other followers. She was a concubine, nothing more. I had no great love for her and neither did any of the disciples. I would gladly trade her life for my brothers any day," he said.

"Did she not carry his child?" Pilate asked. "Did she not marry him?"

"She carried his abomination and lost it, thank

God. We had hoped that she would be killed in Asia. Unfortunately, she was spared by the skill of James' sword."

"If I am any judge of character, I can tell you this, the bargain you have struck with the Emperor is unholy. You will not gain from it and you will suffer for the rest of your days. If your brothers are similar then you deserve each other. I suspect that your life and theirs will be shortened more quickly than you expect."

Caligula's Justice

More than a year ago, my wife, Procula, died. She never forgave me for my part in the rabbi's crucifixion. Of course, I did not reveal to her my involvement in saving him. We were not close. Our arranged marriage was for political reasons, and we bore no personal expectations from the union. The advantages brought increased status in our social circles in Rome, which satisfied us.

I was not a devoted husband because of my military career, but I do not think she cared. My time away got longer and the distance between grew with each passing year. We were civil with each other most of the time, but after the crucifixion, Procula did not have anything good to say to me. I had not known she was a devoted follower and convert until the last months of her life.

When I received my post in Judea, she stayed in Rome. When Caligula exiled me, she had to follow me to Gaul. This made her bitter. Many of our arguments centered on my not managing to keep my post in Judea, which allowed her to stay among her friends and family in Rome. After we arrived in Vienne, she *confided in me. Perhaps she felt comfortable because we were in exile. I could do little to harm her reputation. It was still unpopular to expound on being a Christian follower. The irony is that later, I also became a convert.*

Vienne is perfect for a hermit. It was mostly rural, and farming and fishing were the main topics of discussion with the locals at the village inn. I was bored. There was little to do but drink myself into a stupor. I missed arguing with Procula. Our almost daily battles kept my mind from going completely dormant. Conflict, in any form, was familiar to me and I easily accommodated my wife. After several months, I began to write letters to Rome, inquiring from the friends still left to me the latest news and events in the capital.

This was how I learned of the fate of the rabbi's followers. All but a few fell under the swift hand of Caligula's justice. What Caligula could not complete, he turned over to Claudius and his successor, Nero. These tyrants were his equals in both madness and brutality.

Bartholomew was found skinned alive and beheaded in a ditch. That is not something I would have condoned even during my worst acts of vengeance. Those in Asia are barbarians for the most part, so it was not so surprising.

It is unfortunate for his followers that the rabbi's message sent them into unfavorable surroundings with the Gentiles. The hand of Caligula assassinated some of the disciples. At the same time, the others were victims at the hands of the angry and faithless. Unlike Jerusalem, many Gentiles were less tolerant of the presence of prophets.

Simon the Zealot and Jude were stoned to death in Mauritaine while healing the sick and passing the spirit to those who wanted it. As they professed possessing God's spirit during their preaching, their intentions were misunderstood and believed suspicious. The people took them to be sorcerers instead of men of goodwill. The frightened crowd turned on them and became violent.

The one called James the Lesser was teaching to a small group of children with their parents in Egypt. Two men appeared from behind and speared him in the back, then from the front and piercing his side. They finally launched the fatal blow through his heart. They left him bleeding like a slaughtered calf as the children ran screaming. His body lay dead in the street for days before it was scraped up because the rotting stench was so bad. His body ended on a heap and burned with the rest of the garbage.

Matthew was having tea in Persia one morning. He planned to speak later in the square, but three assailed him and crushed his skull with a rock. Two of them kicked the rest of the life from his body while the other watched laughing until the body no longer moved. They dragged his carcass out beyond the city where the vultures made a good meal of him.

Phillip died in Phrygia by suffocation, because they cut off his penis and stuffed it down his throat. He could not speak or breathe, and soon died. Thomas was brutally extinguished in Madras. Assassins speared him through the throat so violently they almost cut off his head. Clearly, his killers were unskilled butchers. I also heard one very close to the rabbi, named Andrew, was crucified in Patras.

The new Governor of Judea, Herod Agrippa, murdered James the Just, brother to the rabbi. It was quick. They cut his throat as they would a sacrificial animal. James was a goodhearted man and I respected his skill with the sword. Soon after Peter was arrested and imprisoned in Phyrgia, Paul joined with the other one called Simon Magus to form a new alliance of the Gentile churches in Asia. Later, I learned that Nero had assumed the throne from Claudius and summoned Paul to Rome on charges of sedition and inciting rebellion in the East. His vessel capsized at sea and he was shipwrecked on the isle of Melitas.

I thought that his God had saved him, but then

Nero imprisoned him on his return to Rome. Two years later, Nero beheaded him. Truly, their God is fierce and demanding.

Despite my trepidation regarding the Christian God, I did confirm my conversion to the rabbi's way. One of his disciples, the one called Jude, had come to Gaul on his way to Mauritaine. Jude possessed the witness of their God and baptized me into their faith. My final year in this forsaken country, that I helped subdue with my Roman soldiers, is my last view of the world and my final resting place.

Epilogue

No good deed goes unpunished. Mine was no exception. I was simply an after-thought of Emperor Caligula's misgivings, and the convenient exclusion by Claudius who replaced him. I was Procurator of Judea for ten long years and had little to show for my efforts. I outlasted most who tried to rule that restless and horrible land. Some would say that my approach was less than honorable, but I did what I needed to do to maintain order and justice. Here I sit, a stranger in an even stranger land. I live in a small hovel. It lies just beyond the lake near Vienne in Gaul. I am without slaves or any of the conveniences of the palace in Judea that I had grown accustomed to.

All I have left are my memories, and a few small trinkets from the campaigns I fought for the glory that was once Rome. I have no land, wealth, nor even my military rank and honors. My wife, Procula, has died. Some of those campaigns took place in this place, Gaul. Who knew it would become the last vestige of a broken body that is too tired and aged to care? I can no longer speak with good conscience so highly of that *once held glory I so easily placed above any woman or friend, even my dutiful wife. Bitterness is my only friend and keeps me company.*

Procula was a professed Christian follower before she died, but never met the man that I knew, the remarkable prophet man that started it all. I knew him, yet I never openly professed my admiration. Perhaps he came to know my true feelings from my efforts to plan his escape. He will never know that I, too, have become a Christian.

I wonder what has become of him, and if my acts were those of a Good Samaritan. I saved his life from those who hated him but I lament that my plan allowed such torture and abuse. I could not protect his followers from the actions of those who wanted to persecute him.

In my plan for his survival, I managed to alienate my wife and some of my closest friends. I made him promise never to reveal the details of his escape, not even to the Magdalene or closest followers. Any possibility of discovery would throw away any chance for his continuing mission. In addition, he would have placed his woman and close friends in harm's way.

In retrospect, I was unaware of his true purpose. From what I have learned since my exile, his teaching and impact came to nothing in Jerusalem. He was often insulting to the public and freely spoke his mind.

He did not have many who followed him and often stoned wherever he went, even by his own people.

The real irony is with Paul and Simon Magus. Their efforts to build Christian churches in Asia and later in Rome were successful in the end. After Paul died in Phrygia, Magus carried on in Rome as the false apostle to the Gentiles. Those closest to the rabbi in Jerusalem did not favor Paul or Simon Magus, even from the beginning. From what I understand, the Christian church in Rome does not reflect the rabbi's teachings.

The man I once knew, Paul, whose original purpose was the rabbi's undoing, spent most of his time in Asia with Simon Magus and taught the Gentiles his own version of the prophet's doctrines, and to his advantage. Rome's activities to quell the influence of the prophets created a worse nightmare. I wager those two will become martyrs of Christendom. They intended to build a new Christian church of their own, a religion founded upon the importance of his death and its influence, through an alchemical doctrine of magical rites and rituals. The rabbi spoke more about the glory of life than about the sanctity of death. These doctrines have a Syrian and Babylonian flavor, most likely from the influence of Simon Magus.

As close to the rabbi as his followers professed to be, none of them came to his defense during the trial.

We suspected they hid within the catacombs until it was safe to emerge. I was outraged by their cowardice, but he remained unaffected by their behavior. I wrestle with the idea that his teachings were not strong or impressive enough to change the poor character of those men who followed him. Is it not valid to judge a teacher by the quality of his students?

I decided I will not concern myself with the acts of those weak men. I would rather focus my final years upon this extraordinary man. I am, at the very least, a devoted admirer of the man and what he tried to do. He said to me, "If you do not believe in me, then believe in what I am doing."

As a Roman soldier, I pride myself on being honorable and honest. I fought valiantly on the battlefield and stood my ground even if it meant that it would be my last act. A good soldier measures his value against the decisions he makes and the actions he performs without remorse. A Roman soldier asks himself, is this a good day to die? Above all, there is the honor of serving with all your heart that symbol of the greatest good, the might of the Roman Empire and the Emperor. I always believed that in some small way, I was preserving the best of what man had achieved in a civilization.

All is lost to man, for the Empire is crumbling. Now that I am exiled from my greatest love, Rome, I see this clearly. In this I find myself similar to the prophet man. He did his best for the greatest good, but it still falls like pearls at the feet of swine. Like he, if I place myself next to him for a moment, I see that my efforts have been for naught as well. I served and prostrated myself before a harlot, a mistress empty of honor and too shallow of value to be truly a great Empire.

In Rome, I learned to rank my efforts and value with the successful exploits and achievements of the Empire. Achievements for which I am proud to say I am a Roman citizen. They are the Apian Way and the aqueducts providing fresh water to the heart of Rome from hundreds of leagues distant. There is no match for the advent of the baths, the glory of the Republic through senatorial debate, the Coliseum, and of course, the expansion of the commonwealth to the farthest end of the Empire, through many victorious battles for which I heartily took part.

Yet, in the little time I had with this extraordinary man, I learned that real value comes only from within the spirit. No earthly achievements can compare. The rabbi asked me to consider what good I have brought to bear upon my neighbor and to what extent I have allowed such good to exist within myself. I still struggle over these questions, but I fear to discard them because they have a ring of truth.

I do not care much for what this man Paul speaks, though he offers an oral tradition apart from the Jewish law that prescribes how to eat, to dress, and above all that the male genitals be stripped of the foreskin. I could never abide by the restrictions. I admire the prophet man and what he taught, but I cannot abide by this Jewish way. I am a Roman, not a Jew. I have long since given up as child's folly the Roman gods. I struggle with what I do not see. The prophet man's God and kingdom are larger than life. Yet, there is no graven image of his God I can feast my eyes on, or a temple where I can carry myself to and rest. There is no temple to give burnt offerings at the foot of His altar. The rabbi said, "I can find His temple inside my heart, and further, that I need no intercessor to speak for me," unlike Paul's doctrines. I struggle with this as well, but the rabbi warned me that I should not give up the search for my inner temple and that it should be important above all other concerns.

The unholy bargain the fisherman made with Caligula to track down the prophet's wife came to an unfortunate end. She birthed her children, and after some years had passed, she and the children were found and killed. Caligula overturned his unsavory bargain to preserve the lives of Peter's brethren in exchange for the Magdalene, and killed many of the disciples of the prophet. John was an exception. He went mad and Nero exiled the harmless man to the isle of Patmos. Peter and Paul were saved for last. Paul was Roman and he was beheaded. The fisherman was crucified upside down at his request, an ending that was too good for him.

Once again, the loss of the prophet's wife and children saddens me. Though any news from Asia can often be inaccurate, this time I fear it is true.

I am perplexed when I think of all that happened in my ten years as Procurator. The spiritual cause that the Baptist fought for against Herod and Rome, and what the rabbi sought to teach with such fervor was lost in the roar of the chaos that followed. I see none of them standing and for what?

It reminds me of some of the battles I fought for Rome. When I walked the battlefields and surveyed the dead and dying, not only my troops but also of the enemy, I considered their misfortune of having lost a battle that was of importance to them. Their cause is over, and then what? What does it mean? With battles won and lost, the chaos keeps going. Only the faces, names, and places change. I cannot say how much longer Rome shall hold out. She will do so without my help. I am done here. The rest of my days I will spend to chronicle my adventures, misadventures, and wonder at what life might have been if the prophet man had prevailed.

There is a time for all things to begin and end. Rome's time has come to an end, I fear. I have warned others that perhaps the Goths will overtake her. I have said that Rome lays asleep while her enemies endlessly plot her undoing.

During the rabbi's trial, I wanted to ask him why his God had not taken steps to preserve His ministry and His prophet. He said to me once that he was favored. Yet I see his God did nothing to save him. Had we the chance to debate that issue, I would argue that I saved him. He would have replied that his God had chosen me to act in his stead.

Maybe he was crazy, another lunatic from the desert come to haunt us with impossible dreams of a better life. My mind struggles with yielding to the impossible promise of his God's heaven, but even with the passing of time, his words still set my heart ablaze with unanswered questions that I will no doubt take to my grave.

www.ingramcontent.com/pod-product-compliance
Lightning Source LLC
Chambersburg PA
CBHW031240290426
44109CB00012B/377